THE DIVISIVE STATE OF SOCIAL POLICY

The 'Bedroom Tax', Austerity and Housing Insecurity

Kelly Bogue

First published in Great Britain in 2019 by

Policy Press
University of Bristol
1-9 Old Park Hill
Bristol
BS2 8BB
UK
t: +44 (0)117 954 5940
pp-info@bristol.ac.uk
www.policypress.co.uk

North America office:
Policy Press
c/o The University of Chicago Press
1427 East 60th Street
Chicago, IL 60637, USA
t: +1 773 702 7700
f: +1 773-702-9756
sales@press.uchicago.edu
www.press.uchicago.edu

© Policy Press 2019

British Library Cataloguing in Publication Data
A catalogue record for this book is available from the British Library

Library of Congress Cataloging-in-Publication Data
A catalog record for this book has been requested

978-1-4473-5053-8 hardback
978-1-4473-5056-9 ePub
978-1-4473-5055-2 ePDF

Cover design by Robin Hawes
Front cover image: Alamy
Printed and bound in Great Britain by CPI Group (UK) Ltd, Croydon, CR0 4YY
Policy Press uses environmentally responsible print partners

This book is dedicated to the memory of Maria,
and to all those who are still struggling.

Contents

List of terms and abbreviations

Benefit Cap	Cap on the total amount of benefit that most people aged 16 to 64 can receive. How much a claimant receives may be reduced to ensure the total benefit is not more than the cap amount.
BNP	British National Party
DHP	Discretionary Housing Payment: extra payments for those receiving Housing Benefit, made at the discretion of councils to help with the cost of rent.
DLA	Disability Living Allowance: a tax-free benefit for people with a disability who need help with mobility or care costs. DLA is ending for people who were born after 8 April 1948 and are 16 or over. It will be replaced with PIP. PIP helps with some of the extra costs caused by long-term ill-health or a disability for those aged 16 to 64.
DWP	Department for Work and Pensions: the government department responsible for welfare, pensions and child maintenance policy.
ESA	Employment and Support Allowance: replaced Incapacity Benefit and is granted upon completion of a WCA.
JSA	Job Seeker's Allowance: an unemployment benefit that can be claimed while one is looking for work.
LHA	Local Housing Allowance
NHF	National Housing Federation
PIP	Personal Independence Payment: a disability benefit that is currently replacing DLA. Those migrating onto PIP must undergo an assessment.
PRS	Private rented sector: a classification of UK housing tenure offered by a private landlord.
RSL	Registered social landlord
RTB	Right to Buy
SAR	Shared accommodation rate

Social housing sector	Housing let at below-market rents to those most in need. Councils and not-for-profit organisations (such as housing associations) are the ones who provide social housing.
UC	Universal Credit: a single monthly payment which is in the process of being implemented. UC merges six existing benefits into a single benefit payment.
UKIP	UK Independence Party
WCA	Work Capability Assessment: the medical test used by the DWP to decide whether jobless welfare claimants are entitled to sickness benefits.

Acknowledgements

The primary data that features in this book was gathered during the period 2012–16 as part of a doctoral degree funded by the Sociology Department at the University of Manchester and supervised by Professor Hilary Pilkington and Dr James Rhodes. Both of them are great researchers who taught me so much. There are many good people who helped make this book a possibility, far too many to mention, so I won't. You know who you are, and my heartfelt thanks go to each and every one of you.

I am indebted to all the people who participated in this study. Words fail to do justice to the gratitude and affection I have for you all. I remain hopeful of a better future.

Introduction: the repositioning of social housing and welfare provision

In 2007 the global credit crisis erupted, heralding the most serious economic shock since the Wall Street crash of 1929. It was the result, according to Chossudovsky and Marshall (2010: xvi), 'of institutional fraud and financial manipulation'. In response to the crisis, the British Labour government of the time, led by Gordon Brown (2007–10), focused on preventing the wholesale collapse of the banking sector by 'bailing out' the banks. In a brief resurgence of Keynesian economic theory, the Northern Rock bank was nationalised in early 2008, following a run on the bank the like of which had not been seen in Britain for over a hundred years. Other banks were partly nationalised later in the same year. The Treasury then set out on a path of addressing the budget deficit, which was preventing economic recovery and leading to rising debt and interest payments. Spending cuts aimed to reduce the deficit by half by 2014–15, with Gordon Brown insisting that cuts would not affect front-line services. However, following the 2010 general election, a Coalition government of the Conservative Party and Liberal Democrats, led by David Cameron as Prime Minister, was formed. The new Chancellor, George Osborne, set out a new target to eliminate the deficit completely by 2014–15, accelerating the pace of cuts that had been initiated under Labour and leading Britain into a new 'age of austerity'.

Austerity and welfare reform

The legislative programme presented to the UK Parliament after the 2010 general election set out a number of major reforms to the UK social security system. Following plans set out in *21st Century Welfare* (DWP 2010a) and *Universal Credit: Welfare that Works* (DWP 2010b), the Welfare Reform Act received royal assent on 8 March 2012. The Act represented 'the most radical reshaping of the British welfare system since its introduction post-1945' (Hamnett 2011: 147). As well as tackling the budget deficit, reform of the social security system was justified on the basis that it would make the system fairer, more affordable and better able to tackle 'poverty, worklessness and welfare dependency' (DWP 2010b: 2).

In the wake of the financial crisis, social security and public services became the main targets of austerity programmes across the European Union, while in the UK context the Coalition government's programme of austerity measures cut deeper and harder than those in the US – something which, according to Taylor-Gooby and Stoker (2011: 14), was 'unprecedented'. The austere fiscal strategy in Britain was intended to boost economic growth through a package of tax increases, welfare cuts and Whitehall spending restraint. The June 2010 budget announced changes to the social security system, with Housing Benefit targeted as a key area for reform, due to 'ballooning' expenditure. In the UK, Housing Benefit is the main housing subsidy and both private sector and social sector tenants can apply for the benefit, which provides help towards, or pays 100% of, a claimant's rent. Changes to Housing Benefit included reforms to the way in which Local Housing Allowance (LHA) rates are calculated for Housing Benefit claimants in the private rented sector (PRS). Alongside this, a policy known by a number of names – the Social Sector Size Criteria, 'Under Occupancy Penalty' and the 'Removal of the Spare Room Subsidy' – was announced. These two reforms were implemented in 2013. Further reforms were announced as part of the October 2010 Spending Review, including the extension of the shared accommodation rate (SAR) to most single Housing Benefit claimants in the PRS under the age of 35 (previously the SAR had applied to claimants under the age of 25). In addition, a household Benefit Cap was announced. After coming to power following the 2015 general election, the Conservative Party announced further Housing Benefit changes as part of the July 2015 budget. These changes included the freezing of LHA rates from April 2016 for four years; the removal (with some exceptions) of entitlements to Housing Benefit from young people aged 18 to 21 from April 2017; and a reduction in the household Benefit Cap from £26,000 to £23,000 in London and £20,000 elsewhere. While the Benefit Cap is not strictly a Housing Benefit measure it does result in a reduction of Housing Benefit entitlement where a household has a benefit income above the threshold. The Autumn Statement and Spending Review 2015 brought further announcements that LHA rates would be applied to new claimants entering into tenancies after April 2016, with their Housing Benefit entitlement affected in April 2018, although implementation has been delayed.

The Welfare Reform Act 2012 also introduced the new Universal Credit (UC), which will, when fully rolled out across the country, replace most existing benefits. A key objective of UC is to replace the complex system of benefit arrangements currently in place. UC replaces six benefits: Income-Based Job Seekers Allowance, Income-Related Employment and Support Allowance, Income Support, Child Tax Credits, Working Tax Credits and Housing Benefit. Instead of these different benefits UC will provide a single streamlined payment for those who are eligible (DWP 2010b). At the time of writing the Conservative government have delayed the national roll-out of UC to existing claimants; however, anyone making a new claim for benefits will be enrolled onto UC.

Of this raft of measures, the under-occupation deduction applicable to working-age tenants in the social rented sector proved to be highly controversial and the policy was quickly relabelled in media and public discussion as the 'Bedroom Tax'. The Bedroom Tax was essentially a cut in Housing Benefit for those who lived in council or housing association properties deemed to have more rooms than they required for their household size. Not all those who reside in the social rented sector are subject to the policy and the Bedroom Tax applies only to working-age tenants who are claiming means-tested Housing Benefit. Working-age tenants who require no government help with their rent are not subject to room restrictions. However, the way that social housing is allocated means that those moving within the sector are allocated only to properties with the number of rooms to fit their defined household needs. Therefore it is only when the composition of the household changes *and* if the tenant is in receipt of Housing Benefit that they become subject to the policy.

A stated aim of the under-occupancy restrictions was that it would introduce parity and fairness in the allocation of Housing Benefit, since the same provision around room restrictions already existed for millions of people in the PRS. In the PRS claimants receive Housing Benefit for the cost of their accommodation based upon the reasonable accommodation needs of their households. Therefore, it could be argued, private tenants were already effectively subject to the Bedroom Tax after Housing Benefit was reformed in the private sector with the introduction of LHA rates, rolled out nationally in 2008. In the social housing sector eligible rent levels had not been determined by reference to the size of a claimant's household, and the Coalition government of 2010–15 argued that this situation was inequitable.

Consequently, the Bedroom Tax was seen as introducing fairness and ensuring parity between the two sectors. However, there are crucial differences in the way that the change was implemented for existing tenants in the PRS. Reforms to the way Housing Benefit operated in the private sector and the system of determining LHA rates were not imposed on existing private sector tenants, who were granted transitional protection for up to nine months when the national roll-out of LHA was implemented. LHA rates were again cut after 2010. However, those who were already in receipt of Housing Benefit did not experience any changes unless they had changed address or had a break in their claim. This was intended to give existing Housing Benefit claimants sufficient time to adjust to their new set of circumstances, so there was no retrospective application of the policy. Another crucial difference is the vastly greater numbers of disabled people in the social housing sector, and homes that have been specially adapted.

Because of the way social housing is allocated the social sector contains more vulnerable households than other tenures. In England, 50% of households residing in the social sector have at least one member with a long-term illness or disability and the sector also has a high proportion of lone parents and those on low incomes. Three-quarters (75%) of social renters are in the two lowest income quintiles, as compared to the PRS (43%) and owner-occupiers, where those in the lowest income quintiles comprise 29% (English Housing Survey 2016–17). So, while not all social housing tenants were affected by the Bedroom Tax, those who were comprised a demographic containing a high proportion of people living with ill-health or a disability. In England, 3.9 million households live in what has become known as 'social housing' (CIH 2018). Formerly known as 'council housing', social housing is accommodation provided by a housing association, local authority or other organisation at a below-market rent. The government initially estimated that the introduction of the Bedroom Tax would affect 670,000 Housing Benefit claimants when the policy was implemented (DWP 2012), approximately 66% of whom comprised households with a disabled person. In 2014 this figure was revised down to 478,000, reflective of the fact that many households had been reassessed as not being liable, while some households were no longer claiming Housing Benefit support. According to the Department for Work and Pensions (DWP) (2012), of the households affected by the policy, the biggest group to be hit would be middle-aged tenants whose children had grown up and left home. The policy places an onus on the social housing tenant to act in certain ways, or, as the DWP (2012: 7) states, 'tenants will be able to choose whether to occupy appropriately sized accommodation, or pay towards accommodation which is larger than the needs of their household'.

Targeting cuts at Housing Benefit expenditure was intended to reduce the Housing Benefit bill, which had grown exponentially.

Housing Benefit expenditure had risen from £11 billion in 2000–1 to £21 billion in 2010–11 (DWP 2012: 6). Housing Benefit is a key mechanism enabling those on low incomes to be housed, whether they be sick, disabled, unemployed or under-employed. The enactment of the policy meant a reduction in this support and either the shortfall in rent would have to be made up by the tenant, if they wanted to remain in their home, or they could 'choose' to downsize. The policy was highly controversial because it was viewed as targeting some of the most vulnerable people in society. Critiques of the policy called it cruel, draconian and unworkable. But why did a policy that appeared at first glance to address under-occupation and overcrowding and make better use of social housing stock come under such intense criticism? The answer is that in many areas the smaller properties that people were supposed to downsize to were not available. Housing associations had highlighted this and the government spelled it out in their impact assessment, which stated that in many areas there were 'insufficient properties to enable tenants to move to accommodation of an appropriate size even if tenants wished to move and landlords were able to facilitate this movement' (DWP 2012: 12).

There are strong arguments for addressing under-occupancy in the social rented sector, given the huge demand for this form of tenure. It appeared to be a benign policy that would redistribute social housing more fairly and make better use of the social housing stock. At the same time, those tenants who were impacted could move to accommodation better suited to their needs, or, if they wished to remain in those properties, they could work to improve their finances or absorb the shortfall in benefit. The only problem appeared to be the dearth of smaller properties within the sector for people to downsize to, as this fact alone could act as an impediment to increasing the mobility within the sector that the policy aimed to address. However, there was a fundamental issue which appeared to be overlooked in the policy documents: these properties were people's homes. Further, social tenants reside longer in social housing in comparison to private sector tenants, meaning that many of those affected had potentially lived in their homes and neighbourhoods for decades. As such, the policy had the potential to cause hardship to tenants who wished to remain in their homes, and emotional upheaval and potential displacement for those who did not have the means to pay the shortfall in rent.

For those affected by the policy, the new rules mean that a fixed percentage of the net Housing Benefit will be lost, set at 14% for one extra bedroom and 25% for two or more extra bedrooms (Tate 2012). In monetary terms, the average loss per week in Housing Benefit is

£14.40 for one room. The guidelines state that a separate bedroom is allowed for each of the following:

- a couple;
- an adult (age 16 and over);
- two children (under 16) of the same gender;
- two children of either gender who are under 10 years of age;
- a non-resident overnight carer for the tenant, joint tenant or their partners in the property;
- students and members of the armed forces who intend to live at home on their return;
- a severely disabled child who cannot share a bedroom due to their disability. The child in question must be entitled to the Disability Living Allowance (DLA) care component at the highest or middle rate.

Following a ruling by the Supreme Court in 2016, new exemptions from the policy came into force on 1 April 2017. Judges ruled that in two cases – that of Mrs Carmichael (who could not share a bedroom with her husband because of her disabilities) and the Rutherfords (the grandparents of a severely disabled child who needed an additional room for the child's overnight carer) – had suffered disability discrimination contrary to Article 14 of the European Convention on Human Rights. The new exemptions reflect the ruling, allowing an additional bedroom for disabled children or non-dependant adults who require overnight care and for couples who are unable to share a bedroom for health reasons.

The critiques and controversy

Even before its implementation, concerns about the impact of the Bedroom Tax were raised by charities, housing experts and councils. Social housing landlords braced themselves for the potential impacts of Housing Benefit reform and warned that the policy would 'lead to displacement of tenants, increase homelessness and rent arrears, and reduce lenders' confidence in the sector' (Hollander and Bury 2012). In order to prepare tenants for the changes, social landlords diverted resources and staff to undertake awareness campaigns and deal with anticipated rent arrears (Hollander and Bury 2012). Others warned that the reforms could result in the 'social cleansing' of areas, such as London, where rents are at a premium (Curtis 2012). Opposition to the policy quickly mounted and social media in particular became one arena through which anti-Bedroom Tax groups could campaign against the policy, disseminate information and reach out to those affected. Campaigns were also launched regionally by groups who organised marches and rallies aimed at its abolition.

The removal of the spare room subsidy was quickly relabelled the 'Bedroom Tax', a term that was being used widely by the media. The policy is not a 'tax', but Marsh (2014) notes how labelling it as a 'tax' drew on previous antagonism associated with the Poll Tax, and although the term did not originate with the Labour Party they were quick to commandeer it and went on to pledge abolition of the policy if they won the 2015 election. The Liberal Democrats then passed a motion at their party conference in September 2013 which stopped short of calling for the policy's abolition and called instead for more government action to mitigate the hardship it was creating (Marsh 2014). The UK Independence Party (UKIP), in their 2015 manifesto, also said they would abolish the policy.

The negative impacts of the policy soon became apparent, particularly after a visit to the UK by the United Nations Special Rapporteur on housing, Raquel Rolnik, in 2013. Rolnik reported that affected tenants were experiencing 'tremendous despair', anxiety and stress (Rolnik 2013: 16). After visiting different regions of the UK to talk to those affected, she suggested that the policy was taking the UK backwards in terms of the protection and promotion of the human right to housing, and called for it to be abolished. Rolnik's report was dismissed by the government housing minister at the time as 'a misleading Marxist diatribe' (cited in Marsh 2014: 5). Labour used an Opposition Day Motion in Parliament to move a motion to abolish the policy, but this was defeated by the government. Then, in January 2014, a legal loophole was found which meant that tenants who had been living in their properties and who had been claiming Housing Benefit continuously since 1996 (such as the long-term disabled) should have been exempt (Halewood 2014). The government quickly moved to close this loophole by April 2014.

The policy has been in place now, in 2019, for six years and still courts controversy. To date, the policy has been implicated in the deaths of two people. In 2014, one year after it was implemented, a 53-year-old woman committed suicide. She left a letter blaming the government for the financial stress under which the policy had placed her.[1] More recently, video footage emerged of a 31-year-old man telling homeless outreach workers that he had ended up sleeping rough on the streets of Birmingham after he was subject to the policy. He was later found dead in a city underpass in freezing weather.

Geographic differences

Different regions of the UK have been affected differently by the policy. Wales was the worst affected, as it has proportionally more Housing Benefit claimants than elsewhere in Britain. The population is sparser in Wales, with a housing profile unlike that in other parts of the UK. There is also a shortage of one- and two-bedroom homes to house those who want to downsize, resulting in a struggle to find alternative smaller accommodation. The North West, as well as Yorkshire and Humberside, is also heavily affected (43%), followed by Scotland (33%) and the West Midlands (31%). However, the devolved administrations in Scotland and Northern Ireland have sought to fully mitigate the effects of the policy. The rules on Housing Benefit have traditionally applied in England, Wales and Scotland. However, Scotland has gained powers to vary some aspects of social security measures under the Scotland Act 2016. Although the Scottish Government is opposed to the Bedroom Tax it does not have the power to abolish it and has instead provided local authorities with additional funding for Discretionary Housing Payments (DHP) to fully fund the Housing Benefit deductions.

In Northern Ireland the Welfare Reform (Northern Ireland) Bill 2012 failed to make progress. This prompted the UK Government to introduce the Welfare Reform (Northern Ireland) Act 2015 to provide for the implementation of welfare reform measures in Northern Ireland. This delayed the implementation of the policy until February 2017, at the height of the power-sharing collapse. Nevertheless, in an effort to protect tenants from the policy, politicians of the Northern Ireland Assembly worked to set up a fund to offset the reduction in rent. However, this fund is available only until March 2020. The measures put in place by the Scottish and Northern Ireland administrations have largely protected social housing tenants from the changes. It is only in England and Wales that tenants have felt its full impacts.

The raft of legislation aimed at reducing Housing Benefit expenditure has caused concern, with commentators arguing that the measures could lead to rising rent arrears and possible eviction if tenants are not able to meet the shortfall in their rent. In the PRS, both charities such as Shelter and landlord organisations argued that restricting and freezing LHA rates and extending the SAR would make it more difficult for claimants to access the PRS, particularly in areas of high demand. There are, then, concerns about the future of private and social housing sector tenants as a result of reforms to the Housing Benefit system.

While this book focuses on the impact of just one of these policies, the Bedroom Tax, it reflects on how reductions to Housing Benefit more broadly in both the private and social rented sectors are making it increasingly difficult for those claiming Housing Benefit to access affordable housing. For those who are economically inactive or on low incomes, Housing Benefit is often a crucial element in providing housing affordability. However, new measures to reduce Housing Benefit expenditure in both sectors run the risk of private landlords and housing associations being fearful to rent to those who claim Housing Benefit, as the new reductions leave tenants with a shortfall in income and a rent that they may not be able to afford to pay.

The return of the 'housing question' in Britain

For Britain's working classes, housing has always been a site of struggle, both to access and to afford. The failure of the PRS to adequately address housing need in the Victorian era, and the experience of two world wars, led to state intervention in the housing market in the form of council housing. The creation of the British welfare state in the 1940s reinforced the need for housing in order to address the squalor that many were forced to live in. While the growth of the council housing sector ensured that large swaths of the UK population were decently housed, it was the affluent sections of the working class that benefited, as they could afford the rents that were charged. Until the late 1970s the difference in economic outcomes between council tenants and the rest of the population was small. This gap widened significantly during the 1980s as better-off tenants exercised the 'Right to Buy' their homes and allocation of the remaining stock became increasingly targeted on those with lower incomes. However, the ability of the sector to house those with low or no incomes is being systematically eroded as changes in Housing Benefit policy make the sector increasingly unaffordable.

The Bedroom Tax stood in the vanguard of austerity policies which targeted Housing Benefit, being one of the first welfare reforms to be implemented, but others have followed in its wake. In the years since the enactment of the policy many of those affected by it have faced an ongoing struggle. They have had either to make the decision to remain in their homes and absorb the reduction in rent support, or to attempt to downsize to smaller accommodation. For many, trying to remain in a property they can no longer afford has led to the accumulation of rent arrears, the abandonment of homes and homelessness. While this book focuses on the impact that one social policy has had on those it has affected, it speaks to broader concerns about the state of housing in the UK and the ability of those on low incomes to access it.

For many, social housing is a highly valued resource. It has provided security of tenure, unlike the PRS, where the minimum tenancy length is six months; rents have been significantly lower than in the PRS; and it has provided accommodation that people could remain in indefinitely, putting down roots. As such, there is a high level of residential longevity among those who live in social housing in comparison to private renters. Moreover, as Murie (1997: 445) made clear, 'Council housing in Britain encouraged tenants to stay whatever their social and economic circumstances.' As such, tenants can and do feel secure in social housing, they can take pride in their homes, knowing that, unlike in the private sector, the houses they occupy cannot be sold or removed from them arbitrarily. With the introduction of the Bedroom Tax policy this stability has been undermined. Since its implementation, the policy has impacted negatively on tenants, physically and psychologically, as is evidenced by a range of research that has documented the negative impacts on health and wellbeing (Moffatt et al 2015), and on children and their education (Bragg et al 2015). Alongside this, reports by the UN and charities have expressed concern about the detrimental effect the policy is having on tenants. In this book I build upon previous studies by highlighting the impacts which the policy has on health and wellbeing. Further, I argue that the policy is socially divisive and that this has repercussions within the political arena in the UK. This book is about the impacts of the Bedroom Tax policy on 31 affected social housing tenants living in one neighbourhood. But it speaks to wider concerns about how we house and treat those at the lower end of the class structure. The Bedroom Tax policy has worked, in many cases, to spread fear about home, security, community and social networks. Moreover, it has heightened and encouraged a sense of resource competition among people at a time when the UK's political establishment are viewed as increasingly disconnected from the daily realities of people's lives. Housing and shelter is a fundamental human need – which is the reason why it is an intensely emotive topic. Housing is a political issue, and the struggles over it helped to shape the rise of the Labour Party. It has been used by political parties to win support for their brand of politics and dampen down the appeal of rival parties. In more recent times the struggles around social housing have become a central campaigning tool of the far right.

For Boughton (2018a), the development of council housing represented 'the mark of an upwardly mobile working-class and the visible manifestation of a state which took seriously its duty to house its people decently' – particularly so when the free market and private enterprise failed to provide the affordable homes that people needed. However, the social housing sector has declined, while the private sector is growing in prominence. This situation, working in tandem with cuts and freezes targeted at the Housing Benefit system, is resulting in widespread housing insecurity for many and is increasing child poverty, particularly in the PRS (NHF 2019). While this book focuses specifically on the impacts of the Bedroom Tax policy, it reflects more widely on how cuts to the Housing Benefit system in Britain are reshaping the housing landscape for those on the lowest incomes.

Structure of the book

Chapter 2, 'Life without state-supported housing', takes the reader back to a time when council housing did not exist, focusing attention on the social and political conditions that gave rise to state intervention in the housing market. The purpose of the chapter is to highlight the historic tensions that housing gives rise to, and to remember a time when there was no council housing. It discusses the role that rent support, and later the Housing Benefit scheme, played in enabling council housing to become both accessible and sustainable. Through two world wars and the postwar era beyond, to Britain's so-called 'golden age', it charts the political and social upheavals that led to the residualisation of the social housing sector. Bringing the reader up to the present, it reflects on why council housing became increasingly run down and stigmatised. The final sections of the chapter include a focus on the Welfare Reform Act 2012 and how Loïc Wacquant's theory of advanced marginality is instructive in understanding the retrenchment of the welfare state in the UK. The chapter ends with a note on methods, including an overview of the fieldwork site where this study took place.

Chapters 3, 4, 5 and 6 present a case study of the impacts of the Bedroom Tax. While highlighting the consequences which the policy had for tenants, these chapters urge the reader to keep in mind that this is just one policy among many that are working to increase housing precarity. While the chapters focus on just this policy, they also highlight that the participants in this study are also impacted on by other welfare reforms. Chapter 3, 'Living in a state of insecurity', looks at the policy's impact as it was being implemented, exploring how participants reacted to the policy. It explores the ways it affected individuals and dependent children and led to fuel and food poverty and increasing rent arrears. Chapter 4, 'Social housing insecurity as policy and ideology', focuses on the work of Loïc Wacquant and employs Foucauldian conceptualisations, adopting a more theoretical analytical framework to question how and in what ways the retrenchment of welfare abets the 'reengineering of the state' (Wacquant 2013: 8). In this chapter the analysis turns to the relationship between structure and agency and how increased housing vulnerability impacted on participants, acting to responsibilise them and make them accountable for their own housing provision. The chapter questions the motives of the policy, relating it to the increased drive to end security of tenure in the social housing sector and the ongoing processes that are signalling an end to social housing's capacity to afford tenants a 'home for life'. Chapter 5, 'Divisive social policy: the competition for physical and symbolic resources', details the way in which participants made sense of the policy. This chapter illustrates how a sense of being stigmatised and forcefully removed from a home elicited feelings of shame and anger, fuelling a sense of resource competition for housing at the local level in and between different groups. Chapter 6, 'Community and belonging', raises questions about the concept of 'community' and place attachment in the midst of neoliberal restructuring and ideas around the 'Big Society' by reflecting on the experiences of participants who feel threatened with displacement. The chapter highlights that within this close-knit community the competition around and for social housing is not just imagined but is highly visible as respondents discuss their own and others' movement within the neighbourhood. The key argument running through Chapters 5 and 6 is that increasing housing precarity and the perceived forced displacement of long-standing tenants creates a feeling that their community is being deliberately undermined by forces outside their control. Tenants who must rejoin social housing waiting lists after decades of being securely housed face the reality of the current crisis in social housing, as they can see plainly how a one-bedroom property attracts over 100 applicants. At the local level, where there are close friendship ties within the neighbourhood, the re-allocation of homes is highly visible, which leads to resentment and tension about who belongs and who has the right to belong. Central is the idea of community, of knowing and being known and having firm foundations. When home *and* community are threatened, nativism will manifest and claims to entitlements are staked. These two chapters highlight the ruptures in and between the working-class over access to housing. The final chapter of the book, Chapter 7, 'Housing precarity and advanced marginality in the UK', reflects on the impact of the Bedroom Tax and relates the findings to rising housing precarity more broadly. It aims to highlight that the Bedroom Tax, as a *process* of deepening housing insecurity, has led to a toxic mix of fear and anger. Drawing on a range of current research, the chapter argues that the raft of welfare changes targeted at cutting rent support have led to housing precarity and rising homelessness, theorised as advanced marginality. In turn, the deepening poverty which these cuts are creating, alongside increasing housing inequality, is consigning vast swaths of low–income people to a future where they are becoming increasingly locked out of both the social and private rented sectors. Moreover, by drawing on recent research, the chapter reflects on how the rising undercurrent of anger directed at politicians and various 'others' may have contributed to the political upheavals that characterise the divisive state of politics that is evident in the UK today.

2

Life without
state-supported housing

In order to understand what led the state to intervene in the housing market, this chapter begins by giving an overview of the origins of social housing, focusing on the key moments in its development. This is not a definitive account of the evolution of council/social housing; others such as Ravetz (2001) and, more recently, Boughton (2018b) provide a much more focused, in-depth historical analysis. But it aims to highlight why the council housing sector evolved from being seen as the answer to addressing mass housing shortages to a tenure which arguably, unlike any other form of housing tenure, has become bound up with notions of worklessness and dependency. This is an argument that has been used as justification for the erosion of the rent support which, since the introduction of mandatory rent rebate schemes and, later, the Housing Benefit scheme, has made it possible for many low-income households to remain securely housed. The chapter looks at the struggles, tensions and social problems that inadequate, insecure housing engenders and how changing political ideologies can determine the housing fate of those at the bottom end of the class structure.

The housing question in industrial Britain

When examining the historiography of housing, and for the purposes of this book in particular, written accounts about the development of council housing in Britain cannot be presented without reference to the appalling conditions that characterised housing for the working classes in the century prior to its development. To really understand what drove the state to intervene in the housing market we must go back to the late 18th century, when Britain was experiencing the first throes of the Industrial Revolution and people were moving from rural to urban centres: a time when home-based production gave way to the factory system, and when for industrial workers 'home became, in effect, a dormitory for the brief hours not spent in mill, mine or factory' (Ravetz 2001: 9). This was the age when the resources of the world began to be exploited on a mass scale, expanding the trade in human and natural resources. In the process, the human labour drawn to towns and cities endured terrible housing conditions. In Friedrich Engels' description of Manchester's worker districts, documented in his *The Conditions of the Working Class in England in 1844*, he stated:

> Such is the old Town of Manchester ... I am forced to admit that instead of being exaggerated, it is far from black enough to convey a true impression of the filth, ruin and uninhabitableness, the defiance of all considerations of cleanliness, ventilation, and health which characterise the construction of this single district, containing at least twenty to thirty thousand inhabitants. And such a district exists in the heart of the second city of England, the first manufacturing city of the world. If any one wishes to see how little space a human being can move, *how little air!* – he can breathe, how little of civilisation he may share and yet live, it is only necessary to travel hither. (Engels 1845: 584)

At that time, housing in industrial towns and cities was provided by private landlords, and was of a condition, given the lack of sanitary infrastructure, which by today's standards would be unimaginable. The housing conditions of the working classes who were pouring into urban centres during the Industrial Revolution had been a focus of discourse and agitation since the 1820s. The subject of inadequate housing filled books, pamphlets, government documents and newspaper exposés. Writing in 1883 on the 'housing question' that so fired the indignation of philanthropists, Andrew Mearns produced what some suggest was a tract of significant importance in the context of 19th-century housing reform. In his pamphlet *The Bitter Cry of Outcast London: An Inquiry into the Condition of the Abject Poor*, he described in some detail the housing conditions in one section of south London, where the poor are

> charged for these pestilential dens a rent which consumes half the earnings of a family, and leaves them no more than from 4d. to 6d. a day for food, clothing and fire; a grinding of the faces of the poor which could scarcely be paralleled in lands of slavery and of notorious oppression. (Mearns 1883: 18)

Mearns called for state intervention in the housing market, stating: 'we shall be pointed to the fact that without State interference nothing effectual can be accomplished upon any large scale. And it is a fact. These wretched people must live somewhere' (Mearns 1883: 24). While Mearns's pamphlet was viewed as pivotal in bringing attention and commentary to the issue of deplorable housing conditions, his exposé followed on the back of the work of others who had highlighted the housing conditions of the working classes in print culture.[1] Mearns was describing a situation that was widely known, brought to public attention by earlier writers and reformers. The exponential growth of cities, alongside outbreaks of cholera, had drawn widespread attention to housing conditions, primarily because such poor conditions were associated with disease, as well as criminal, sexual and religious immorality.

It is the case, then, that the seeds of state intervention in housing can be traced back to middle-class intellectuals, reformers and philanthropists as well as working-class radicals and socialists who were agitating for land reform. In 1851 the Chartist Convention set out their commitment to land nationalisation, which they believed would lead to improved housing conditions. Consequently, in their social programme, they called for

> The state to be empowered to purchase land, for the purpose of locating thereon the population, as tenants, individually or in association, paying a rent charge to the state. The funds for each purpose to arise from the rent-charge payable on the common, poor and crown lands above mentioned, and such other sources as may hereafter be determined. (Cited in Bowie 2017: 78)

By the end of the Victorian period significant improvements had taken place regarding public health, but the 'housing question' remained. London's East End, in particular, became a popular destination for 'slumming', where the middle and upper classes could ogle the living conditions of the least well-off. Similarly to the 'poverty porn' of today, where those with the least power and economic resources are subject to the gaze of newspaper and TV audiences, the historical literature was

> little more than a register of revulsion suffused with an Hogarthian grotesqueness and characterised by a fixation upon the pathological, a fascination for the curious. The men of letters or even the more hard-nosed quantifiers, compilers of blue books and the like – moral statisticians,

as they liked to regard themselves – were in this respect barely distinguishable. The working man, it was generally agreed, was a rather brutish creature insensitive and without culture, a fugitive from an Arnoldian nightmare, who had to be moralised lest civilisation be trampled beneath the weight of his barbarous boot. (Englander 1979: 12)

In much of the historically recorded literature on housing, the voices of those who experienced appalling housing conditions are often silent. As in all things, it is those with the most social, economic and political power who get to speak on behalf of those with little. But, where their voices are discernible, the sentiment expressed draws parallels with the voices of today, as will become clear in later chapters. What kept slum dwellers in their slums was a lack of housing and the unaffordability of the housing that did exist, with the private sector unable to provide the amount of homes needed for the rapidly expanding cities and their growing populations. Looking back at the historical record we can see common themes and sentiments around the housing question that resonate today and which form the core themes of this book. The territorial stigmatisation of poor neighbourhoods, the perception that poverty was a result of individual actions and the inequality that divided the working-class from the rest of society persist in present-day Britain. Housing and class are intimately linked, as those at the bottom of the class structure still have few options and choices over the type of dwellings they inhabit. What links the past and the present in regard to the housing question of that time and the housing question that has again reared its head in modern-day Britain is the ability of those on low incomes to access housing that they can afford to rent.

The ability to pay the rent and the fear engendered when faced by an inability to do so induce the same anxiety today as they did in the 1800s. The combined effects of poor housing and unaffordable rents persist in their adverse effects on physical and mental health, never more so than when rent arrears accumulate and eviction looms large. In Englander's *Landlord and Tenant in Urban Britain: The Politics of Housing Reform, 1838–1924*, he describes how,

> To less adventurous sorts arrears imposed a crushing burden on body and soul. Besides going without adequate diet, there was always the dreadful uncertainty as they tried not to contemplate the future. 'I'm expecting notice to quit every Monday; and when the collector comes I feel I could

sink through the floor', said one wife desperately trying to pay off £2 arrears. (Englander 1979: 37)

The inability to meet rent payments was a constant source of struggle. Even when new housing was made available, it was the better-off section of the working class who could access it and afford to pay the rents being charged.

The problem of rent

During the 1880s, debates about the condition of housing led to greater concern, and a Royal Commission on the Housing of the Working Classes was established which led to the enactment of the Housing of the Working Classes Act in 1885. This was a public health Act which gave local authorities the power to condemn slums, but not to purchase land and build. This came later with the Housing of the Working Classes Act 1890, which empowered London's local councils to build houses as well as to clear away slums. Britain's first public housing development, one of the oldest council estates, the Boundary Street estate in Bethnal Green, London, was built on the site of the 'old Nichol rookery'. This was the most infamous slum in London, an area written about by Arthur Morrison in his *A Child of the Jago* (1896). Although the ideal was to rehouse the former residents of the 'old Nichol' in the new Boundary Street properties, the rents being charged were too high and only a fraction of those displaced returned. Writing about the demolition of the slum and the erection of the new estate, Morrison stated:

> The houses of the Old Jago have been pulled down, the Jago difficulty has been cleared out of the way. That is far from being the case. The Jago, as mere bricks and mortar, is gone. But the Jago in flesh and blood still lives, and is crowding into neighbourhoods already densely over-populated. (Morrison 1896: 5)

Building new homes did not address the problem of rent unaffordability. But the Victorian legacy of housing concern eventually led to more concerted state intervention, mainly as a result of concern around disease and public health. Nevertheless, an increase in housing legislation made little impact on the housing conditions of those on low incomes, and agitation and division festered. The Housing of the Working Classes Act 1890 made little impact, being merely a consolidation of previous Acts as a result of the outrage over *The Bitter Cry*. Overcrowding and rent struggles continued and families displaced by redevelopment had little choice but to enter the workhouse, where their families were broken up (Englander 1979).

Politically, the housing question remained a marginal issue, and continued so until the advent of the First World War in 1914. Throughout 1915 unrest grew, aggravated by rising rents which had resulted in the eviction of servicemen's wives. Indeed, as rising rents began to affect the 'respectable' working-class, anger grew as they were confronted with the prospect of eviction, something that was viewed as affecting only the 'disreputable' poor. Rent strikes ensued, notably in Glasgow, but also in other areas of the UK. Munitions workers flocking to industrial centres found a lack of housing to accommodate them, which added to the tension. While the better-off working-class became active in the various tenants' associations that appeared at this time, the poor residing in slums responded in their own way. At street level, poorer slum-dwelling tenants who were under pressure of rising rents and the threat of eviction responded by withholding rents, intimidating rent collectors and doing 'moonlight flits' (secretly leaving the property) to avoid eviction and the payment of arrears (Englander 1979). That is, they responded to the threat of being put out onto the street or entering the workhouse in the only way they could: with anger. The effect of industrial fatigue and food shortages exacerbated tensions even further. Englander (1979: 382) highlighted how, in Barrow, the expression of resentment was targeted at Belgian refugees who were employed at Vickers shipbuilding yard and who had purchased property, which would result in the eviction of the sitting tenant. Englander cites a local magistrate in Barrow who warned the minister of munitions:

> As sure as you and I are here there will be Satan's own row if Belgian people are allowed to buy houses and the working classes in Barrow-in-Furness are turned out into the streets. There will be a riot, I feel sure. (Englander 1979: 382)

Around the same time, workers were organising, demanding the extension of the vote and better working conditions and pay. The resentment and anger around housing found an outlet in the corresponding rise of the Independent Labour Party in which key figures were involved such as John Wheatley, who became the Minister for Health in the Labour government that rose to power in 1924. Industrial unrest gained momentum, aggravated by poor diet, poor labour conditions and bad housing. And the war-time Coalition government took note, appointing a commission of inquiry into industrial unrest in 1917. The inquiry report clearly showed that housing was a major contributory factor underpinning disturbances, and accused the Independent Labour Party and the Central Labour College Movement of spreading propaganda as a means to capitalise on the widespread discontent.

The state takes action

The conclusions of the Commissioners' report into industrial unrest stated that public disturbances 'can only be allayed by the Government taking steps to grapple with a problem which appears to have grown too great for private enterprise now to meet'.[2] With the end of the war in sight, the Prime Minister, David Lloyd George, added impetus to the call for concerted state intervention on housing when he stated:

> The problem of housing in this country is the most urgent that awaits solution ... We have talked about it, we have played with it for forty or fifty years. But it has never really been taken in hand. We have acts running into hundreds and hundreds of sections. We have had regulations that would fill a library. We have had the most attractive pictures of model dwellings ... But you cannot plough the wasteland with forms. You cannot sweep away slums with paper and you cannot cope with the wants of the people with red tape. (Lloyd George, quoted in Wilding 1972: 326)

After the war ended, the Housing and Town Planning Act 1919 was enacted, otherwise known as the Addison Act after its key architect, the Minister for Health, Dr Christopher Addison. Politically, at this juncture in history there was cross-party consensus that the state needed to intervene in housing as part of postwar reconstruction and to quell the rising tension that those in power feared could result in a working-class revolution. However, key problems arose over who would have financial responsibility for housing development, and for how long responsibility would lie with local authorities. These issues were slow to be resolved, and progress on house building stalled as local authorities sought to limit their financial liability. But progress was made, and in this period council housing provided homes for the relatively high-status, skilled working-class, and the interwar years

1919–39 saw a greater amount of council house building, providing on average 50,000 dwellings a year (Alcock and May 2014).

The importance of the Housing and Town Planning Act 1919 is not in what it achieved in terms of providing homes, but in what it represented: the first large-scale government intervention in building houses for the working classes. After 1930, local authorities began to focus on slum clearance and redevelopment, but by the beginning of the Second World War over a million council houses had been built (Malpass and Murie 1999). However, there was no political consensus that the council housing sector would be a large or permanent answer to the housing problem (Forrest and Murie 1988).

The welfare state and the council estate

The experience of two world wars had highlighted issues of social injustice and shifted attitudes about the causes of poverty and inequality, leading to the founding of the welfare state (Titmuss 1950). William Beveridge, the author of the Beveridge Report (1942), on whose blueprint the welfare state was founded, identified five 'giants': poverty, disease, ignorance, squalor and idleness. Beveridge proposed setting up a welfare state with social security, a national health service, free education, council housing and full employment to tackle them. Following this, the postwar period saw the largest house-building programme ever undertaken in the UK. Following the destruction wrought by the Second World War, in the two decades after the war almost three million local authority homes were built (Alcock and May 2014). As Dorling (2014: 38) has noted, the period from 1945 to 1970 'is now famous for alternating Labour and Conservative administrations vying to demonstrate which could build the most state housing'.

Economically, the period from 1950 ushered in what many referred to as Britain's 'golden age', with rapid economic growth, low unemployment and low and stable inflation. But poverty persisted, and while council housing became a key part of the postwar settlement, rents were still unaffordable for many on low incomes.

In response to rent strikes and the threat of industrial action in support of them during the First World War, the war-time government had been forced to introduce rent controls. After the war government subsidies were introduced to aid local authorities to build general-needs council housing to rent at below-market levels. However, the rents being charged were still out of reach to all but the better-off sections of the working class. Moreover, discriminatory allocation policies ensured the exclusion of those on the lowest incomes, as well as of female-headed households and ethnic minority groups (Bradley 2014). In the 1930s rents were raised and council house subsidies were redirected towards slum clearance, and means-tested rent rebates were made available. These changes in policy resulted in intra-class struggles over council housing. More affluent tenants felt aggrieved that that they were paying higher rents to subsidise rent rebates for the least well-off. Tenants' organisations reacted by taking to the streets in a series of rent strikes, notably in Leeds and Birmingham (Ravetz 2001). Before 1939, evictions for non-payment of rent left tenants to the vagaries of the old workhouse system or the Public Assistance Committee. However, by 1939 there were a variety of differential or rebated rent schemes, but their availability was haphazard because many local authorities chose not to implement them.

After the Second World War the Labour Party won the 1945 general election in a landslide victory. Enthusiastic supporters of the Beveridge Report, they enacted the National Insurance Act 1946, which created the structure of the welfare state. In outlining his scheme for National Insurance Beveridge had found 'the problem of rent' to be a significant issue. He dedicated a chapter to it in his report (Beveridge 1942), and grappled with three characteristics which made it difficult to calculate the level of rent that would be included in social security benefits. Beveridge noted firstly that rent levels varied from region to region; secondly, that rent levels differed within the same geographical area; and thirdly, that families of similar size and income paid different levels of rent (Nevitt 1977). Significantly – and this had been the case in the past as much as in the present – during times of unemployment rent still needed to be paid and could not be reduced in the same way as other household expenditure could. Taken together, it was these facts that made it difficult to calculate one universally appropriate level of benefit, and for that reason rent was not covered as part of National Insurance benefits. The National Assistance Act 1948, while formally abolishing the Poor Law system, established provision for those who did not pay National Insurance contributions. Those left uncovered by the 1946 Act could apply for rent support from the National Assistance Board, which replaced the Public Assistance Committees (Ravetz 2001).

The use of rent rebates expanded in the 1960s, and in 1972 the Housing Finance Act made means-tested assistance mandatory. Legislation enacted in 1973 also provided rebates or allowances for low-income tenants in the private sector. Kemp (2007) notes that these 'housing additions' to social assistance were left relatively unchanged until the system of rent rebates and allowances was replaced by a single

Housing Benefit scheme in 1982. Housing Benefit was paid directly to landlords, providing rent support for those on low wages, tapering off as wages rose, and a 100% rent subsidy for tenants on Income Support. Growing reductions in government subsidies for housing, alongside the removal of private sector rental controls, led to rent increases. These increases in rent had a knock-on effect on Housing Benefit expenditure. The rising costs of Housing Benefit became a major issue for subsequent governments, as the move to subsidise people rather than 'bricks and mortar' led to a decline in council house building and more people looked to the private sector for housing, where rents were, on average, higher. In 1978–79 Housing Benefit expenditure was around £3 billion, but as claimant numbers rose and rent controls were removed from the late 1980s onwards expenditure continued on an upward trajectory, reaching £25 billion by 2013–14.

The development of public housing after the Second World War was characterised by the council estate. The postwar demand for housing meant that cities expanded their boundaries, building estates on the periphery where land was available. By the end of the war, and given the scale of the destruction wrought by the bombing of British cities, it was estimated that four million new houses were needed, while millions more remained unfit for human habitation (Grindrod 2013). The postwar reconstruction of Britain began. The council estate, which would be bemoaned in later years for a whole host of society's social, economic and moral ills, in much the same way as the poor of Britain's Victorian slums were, became the shining beacon of peace and of hope in a more equitable future for the working classes. Although the idealistic underpinnings of these estates were inspired by the Garden City movement, or cottage-style planned communities, the techniques often used to construct them relied on factory-built components that used large panel system techniques, comprising prefabricated concrete sections. Many of the new estates sought to mimic the Radburn layout. Pioneered in New Jersey in the US in the 1930s, the Radburn layout was hailed as the answer to the needs of a 'modern city', where the automobile added a new dimension to urban living. The Radburn layout promised to deliver 'the town for the motor age' (Alexander 2009).

Initially, housing on these new estates was let to households from slum-clearance areas, giving preference to those who upheld an image of respectability and cleanliness. As a result, many in acute housing need were denied access to the council housing sector – a situation that Ken Loach brought to public attention in 1966 with his film *Cathy Come Home*. In later years the Housing and Homeless Act 1977 and the Race Relations Act 1976 widened access to the sector for people of colour and lone mothers, and placed a statutory homeless duty on local authorities. Arguably, the provision of rent rebates and, later, the Housing Benefit system enabled many low-income groups such as the homeless and single parents to access and afford council housing. However, British citizens who arrived in the UK from the Commonwealth, such as the so-called 'Windrush Generation', invited to the UK between 1948 and 1971, like other waves of migrants before and after them faced discrimination in the housing market. The sector still continued to privilege the 'respectable' white working class, as the actions of housing officials served to restrict minority ethnic access to the best housing. Henderson and Karn's (1987) study of council housing allocation in Birmingham, conducted between 1977 and 1982, focused closely on the allocation system in the years of slum clearance. They found that ethnic minority households were consistently allocated the worst council housing, often in the inner city with the oldest and most dilapidated housing stock. Access to the sector was also hindered by requirements for applicants to have lived in an area for a period of time in order to qualify for social housing (Rex and Moore 1967). Attempts to address racial disadvantage and discrimination led to the creation of a Black and Ethnic Minority housing sector in the 1980s. Throughout the 1970s council house building slowed down, and the election of Margaret Thatcher's Conservative Party in 1979 was to mark a decisive turning point in the future of council housing.

Thatcher, neoliberalism and the privatisation of public housing

Margaret Thatcher came to power amid the global capitalist crisis of the 1970s. From 1973, global economic shocks and the oil and energy crisis resulted in economic stagnation and industrial decline. Against the backdrop of these macroeconomic crisis conditions, the postwar consensus embodied in the Keynesian welfare state and collectivism broke down. In its place neoliberalism rose to prominence as an economic–political project. The emergence of neoliberalisation in the UK can be traced back to the 1970s, when neoliberal think-tanks such as the Institute for Economic Affairs became influential among Conservative politicians (Harvey 2005). In 1979 Margaret Thatcher was elected Prime Minister and began reforming the economy by abandoning Keynesianism in favour of 'supply side' monetarism. This neoliberal turn involved attacking social solidarity and trade unions, which were seen as hindering competitive flexibility, further rolling back the welfare state and privatising social housing (Harvey 2005). Neoliberalism is a problematic concept within the social sciences; broadly defined, it has a number of key features which embody the principles of privatisation, deregulation and small government. Peck and Tickell view neoliberalism as a process, which they refer to as neoliberalisation. They summarise how,

> in contrast to the Fordist-Keynesian golden age, when the national-state became the principal anchoring point for institutions of (gendered and racialized) social integration and (limited) macro-economic management, neoliberalization was inducing localities to compete by cutting social and environmental regulatory standards and eroding the political and institutional collectivities upon which more progressive settlements had been constructed in the past. (Peck and Tickell 2002: 385)

In the UK neoliberalism was exemplified in the privatisation of council housing and the enactment of the Right to Buy (RTB) legislation, ushered in as part of the Housing Act 1980. In addition to the rapid continuation of the transfer of local authority council housing stock to registered social landlords (RSL) in the late 1980s, the decision to introduce RTB represented a defining moment in the evolution of council housing. As suggested by Hodkinson et al (2013: 4), it was arguably 'one of the most iconic and significant applications of neoliberal policy worldwide and has been central to the transformation of UK society over the past three decades'.

The RTB policy gave sitting council tenants huge discounts if they chose to buy their homes, with a resale restriction of five years, later reduced to three years. Funds generated through RTB could not be used by local authorities to replace the homes that had been sold, which resulted in a reduction in the size of the sector. Increasing stock transfer to RSL meant that 'council housing' became more widely known as 'social housing'. While RTB depleted the available stock of social housing, the processes that constituted the residualisation of the sector involved a number of key aspects (Pearce and Vine 2014). Allocation systems prioritised those most in need as the sector was contracting, which in turn changed the characteristics of social housing tenants as the most desirable stock was sold off (Harloe 1995). Further, as the stock was sold off and not replaced, the sector became increasingly associated with poor-quality housing (Pearce and Vine 2014).

The idea of selling off council housing to sitting tenants did not originate with Thatcher, as existing legislation had included provision for local authorities to sell to sitting tenants. However, the RTB represented a decisive shift and, as Hodkinson et al suggest, the implementation of this 'neoliberal project' was 'aimed at transforming the entire housing system, not simply privatizing the existing public stock and ending the role of the state in directly meeting housing need' (Hodkinson et al 2013: 4). Thatcher's 'property owning democracy' became the principal housing objective, and the scheme was driven in part by the desire to ensure electoral advantage and to sever the relationship between living in a council house and voting Labour. As Lund (2016: 126) makes clear, 'housing tenure has a long history as a local political battleground', and it remains a battleground today. The policy was seen by some Conservative strategists as a way to weaken the appeal of the Labour Party. Michael Heseltine was the minister responsible for the Housing Act 1980 and he made sure to close all known loopholes to its implementation so as to stave off resistance from Labour-controlled authorities (Lund 2016). Security of tenure for council tenants was also included in the Act. Lund (2016: 129) describes this as a 'masterstroke' as it made 'council house sales an individual right vested in a "secure tenant" – a new tenancy status for the council tenant – rather than an obligation on authorities to sell to tenants'. Among better-off council tenants, the scheme proved massively popular.

Thatcher's RTB policy left a lasting legacy. Over two million homes were sold under the scheme. The policy has also contributed to the increase in private landlordism, as nearly 40% of these homes are now being let in the PRS (Barker 2017). While the scheme benefited individuals, it had a collective cost insofar as the best council properties were sold and future generations were denied access to social rents, adversely affecting the ability of those on low incomes to access the sector. As it stands, there are over a million people languishing on social housing waiting lists – and that leaves uncounted those who are not even eligible to apply. As the council housing sector contracted, more households became reliant on finding accommodation in the insecure PRS.

Significantly, the RTB scheme had an adverse impact on Housing Benefit levels, which continued to rise. As Thatcher's and subsequent administrations reduced levels of house building, Housing Benefit became the principal means through which tenants on low incomes could afford to be housed. The growth of the PRS alongside the retraction of the council housing sector has helped to inflate the Housing Benefit bill. Fewer people living in social housing and paying social rents means that more are going into the PRS and paying a higher, market rent. Moreover, those properties acquired through RTB and which are now being rented in the private sector may be exacerbating the rise in Housing Benefit expenditure. As Sprigings and Smith suggest:

> The higher rents in the PRS have always been known but it seems likely that meeting the housing needs of low income households in former council housing costs the Department for Work and Pensions (DWP) over £1bn per year in additional Local Housing Allowance (LHA) supporting the difference between council rents (that would have been charged to these tenants if they had been living in council stock) and the market rents of the PRS. (Sprigings and Smith 2012: 59–60)

Further, the situation has been exacerbated by the rising levels of working households claiming Housing Benefit, which have more than doubled since 2008, representing 17% of all Housing Benefit claimants (Webb 2012). More people are claiming Housing Benefit because stagnating wages and the huge rise of insecure employment result in falling incomes.

New Labour and council housing

By the time New Labour gained electoral victory with a landslide election result in 1997, the council housing sector had suffered from decades of disinvestment. New Labour continued with the previous Conservative government's policy of supporting the transfer of council housing stock to housing associations. It also inherited a council housing sector with a backlog of repairs needed to its properties. The decline and disrepair of estates led to concerns around rising levels of social exclusion which became focused on run-down estates rather than the continuing legacy of deindustrialisation and changes in the economy that had led to increasing poverty of opportunity. Reflecting New Labour's concern with social exclusion, and in a gesture that linked the concept to the council estate and notions of a British 'underclass', Tony Blair made his first speech as Prime Minister in 1997 at the Aylesbury housing estate in London, where he stated:

> There is a case not just in moral terms but in enlightened self-interest to act, to tackle what we all know exists – an

underclass of people cut off from society's mainstream, without any sense of shared purpose. (Blair 1997, cited in Lund 2007: 16)

RTB legislation, alongside needs-based allocation systems, also had the effect of concentrating lower-income households within a smaller council housing sector. By the time New Labour came to office in 1997 the image of council housing had become tainted. The postwar 'golden age' that followed the Second World War until 1973 could also apply to the erstwhile council estate in terms of its image. The residualisation of the sector and the growing concentration of lower-income households blighted by the loss of industries and long-term unemployment provided fertile ground for the growth of the drug economy amid the economic and social upheavals of the 1970s and 1980s. Council estates and, increasingly, the households residing in them were blamed for the structural changes taking place. They increasingly began to be seen as 'problem' places in the popular and political imagination and, as the years went on, an association between council estates, benefit claimants and welfare state dependency grew. This was fuelled by discourses about Britain's rising 'underclass' propagated by the work of Charles Murray and his assertion, put forward in 1990 in his book *The Emerging British Underclass*, that Britain had a growing underclass fostered by state benefits. Iain Duncan Smith, the former Conservative Party leader and the man who would champion the Welfare Reform Act 2012 in his later cabinet post as Secretary of State for Work and Pensions, visited the Easterhouse estate in Glasgow in 2002. Duncan Smith was pictured on the estate looking close to tears. Afterwards he stated:

> Standing in the middle of an estate like Easterhouse, you know it was built after the war for a purpose, only to see this wrecked and dreadful set-up today, with families locked into generational breakdown, poverty, drug addiction and so on. And that really does confront you with the thought that we did this – we built the brave new world, and look where it's gone. It was a sort of Damascene point. It's not that I wasn't thinking about these things before, but after Easterhouse I saw that we had to do something about it. (Quoted in Derbyshire 2010)

Duncan Smith went on to help establish the Centre for Social Justice in 2004, in order to 'put social justice at the heart of British politics and make recommendations to tackle the root causes of poverty'.[3]

In the meantime, New Labour's approach to council housing was focused on improving the existing stock rather than funding new builds, as well as introducing initiatives to address 'social exclusion'. The then Prime Minister, Tony Blair, advocated a new brand of 'third way' politics which, simply defined, occupied a political position between 'New Right' Conservatism and the 'Old Left' of Labour (Levitas 2005). However, some have argued that New Labour drove forward the project of neoliberalisation by embracing the new era of marketisation (Jessop 2007; Ruskin 2010). New Labour adopted a similar approach to council housing by embracing the role of housing associations as a 'third arm' of housing provision (Lund 2016). The promotion of stock transfers intensified and, despite the efforts of anti-stock transfer campaigns such as that established by Defend Council Housing, many tenants favoured a 'yes' vote in ballot transfer campaigns in which they could vote for or against transferring their local authority homes to Housing Associations. This was particularly the case where housing associations held out the prospect of carrying out much-needed improvements to the stock after years of under-investment. The result was that 'almost a million dwellings were removed from local authority ownership via transfers and by 2010, there were no council houses in almost half the local authorities in England and Wales' (Lund 2016: 195). For many local authorities, stock transfer was seen as the only way to ensure the substantial reinvestment in the sector that was so badly needed (Cowen and Marsh 2001). Concerns around social exclusion were also being raised in policy documents emanating from the government's Social Exclusion Unit which laid out a comprehensive strategy for neighbourhood renewal as a way to tackle deprivation and exclusion. Among other initiatives this saw the implementation of the 'Decent Homes' programme, neighbourhood renewal schemes, the 'new deal' for communities and the roll-out of Sure Start schemes in disadvantaged neighbourhoods. Alongside these initiatives, the regulation of social housing tenants intensified under New Labour with the introduction of Anti-Social Behaviour Orders.

A series of government-funded programmes aimed to address the physical deterioration and management of estates, some of which had empty or unlettable properties. At the same time specific social groups, such as lone parents, who in the 1970s had been viewed as a group facing significant levels of deprivation, were morally condemned, and this was fuelled by media debate around benefit 'scroungers' (Jacobs et al 2003). Lone parents were given preferential status in allocation systems because they were viewed as a priority needs group, but this led to accusations that single women were deliberately becoming pregnant in order to secure a social housing tenancy. These representations proliferated in the context of growing Housing Benefit expenditure (Jacobs et al 2003). From the 1970s onwards the council housing sector, Ravetz (2001: 238) argues, was 'obliged to accept people that it would previously have excluded and, with a shrinking and deteriorating stock, it was forced into a role it had never been intended for, as "housing for the poor"'. The stereotyping of council housing and estates is best captured by Mooney (2008: 14) when he observes that council/social housing estates became increasingly characterised in the popular media as places 'where "benefit" and "dependency" cultures endure, and in which crime and delinquency apparently flourish'.

However, these sweeping stereotypes of council housing and council estates failed to acknowledge their successes, including lower rents and greater security than the PRS. Furthermore, the sector can act as a refuge for those facing complex and long-standing problems. As Cole (2007) points out, the massive demand for this form of tenure is testament to its ongoing appeal, and the representation of the social housing sector as a tenure which acts as an impediment to social and economic mobility and which fosters benefit dependency is a 'common sense' assertion that does not stand up to empirical scrutiny. The concept of 'welfare dependency', while featuring prominently in political and public discourse, is problematic. Fraser and Gordon (1994) note that the term 'dependency' has been used to frame debates about poverty and inequality in the US and carries connotations of contempt and stigma. In the UK context, welfare dependency rhetoric has been used as a discursive strategy to draw attention away from structural inequalities and the causes of poverty, recasting those who seek assistance from the social security system as lacking personal and social responsibility (Wiggan 2012; Garrett 2015).

For many of those whose lives could have been much harsher without the support of the state and the shelter afforded by council housing, a different picture is discernible. Writing in the preface to his book *Austerity: The History of a Dangerous Idea* (Blyth 2013), the political scientist Mark Blyth reflects on how council housing afforded him shelter, while the social security system prevented him from experiencing hunger. While recognising that he may be an extreme example of intergenerational social mobility, he poignantly expresses his fear that the undermining of the social security system through austerity cutbacks may make it harder for future generations like his to benefit from the security it provided. As he states:

> What made it possible for me to become the man I am today is the very thing now blamed for creating the crisis itself: the state, more specifically, the so-called runaway, bloated, paternalist, out-of-control, welfare state. (Blyth 2013: 9)

The fact that millions of homes were sold to sitting tenants as a result of the RTB attests to the fact that many households have been satisfied with their council homes. Moreover, despite the challenge the sector has faced, Cole and Furbey (1994: 174), in their research, found a 'genuine commitment' among many council tenants. Nevertheless, in 2006 the Smith Institute published a collection of essays under the title *Rethinking Social Housing*. The introductory comments expressed by the editors suggested that social housing policies and practices established under welfarist foundations were no longer fit for purpose in the context of a growing global economy. They argued against the 'homes for life' approach, setting the tone for the subsequent essays which appeared in the report and which, among other subjects, dealt with such issues as 'Social housing isn't working', 'Breaking up dependency on existing estates' and 'Flexible tenure neighbourhoods'. Moreover, they advocated 'action to dismantle "social" estates' in order 'to break up existing concentrations of deprivation in every local authority in the UK, beginning with estates dominated by social housing' (Dwelly and Cowans 2006: 82). This document could be said to spell out a road map of what was to follow after the financial crash and the change of government which followed the 2010 general election.

The Coalition government and the Welfare Reform Act 2012

The financial crisis of 2007–8 led many commentators to declare the demise of the neoliberal ideology that had risen to prominence under the administrations of Thatcher in the UK and Reagan in the US. However, rather than collapse, neoliberalism was reconfigured after the 'long winter of Keynesianism', which immediately followed (Blyth 2013: 17). Neoliberal ideas of deregulation, privatisation, state and welfare state retrenchment re-emerged, and were revived under the banner of austerity (Blyth 2013). Austerity, the policy of cutting the state's budget to promote growth, became the new order of the day with the election of the Conservative-led Coalition government in 2010. Blyth (2013) notes that neoliberalism, also known as the 'Washington Consensus', incorporates a list of policies which include fiscal discipline, reordering public expenditure priorities, tax reform, liberalising trade and foreign direct investment, privatisation and deregulation. These comprise the essential features of neoliberalism, and also happen to be the essential features, Blyth (2013: 161) argues, 'of what we now call austerity politics'.

The scale of the deficit after the economic crash of 2007–8 meant that reducing the national debt became the dominant theme of the 2010 general election. The Coalition government promised to tackle the deficit by reducing spending rather than increasing taxes (Lund 2016). Their approach to social housing found expression in the passage of the Localism Act 2011. The Act made a number of significant reforms to the social rented sector, including reforming allocation processes so that those deemed not to be in need could be prevented from joining the waiting list. It also reformed homelessness legislation so that local authorities could house homeless applicants in the PRS. Significantly, it gave social landlords the power to introduce flexible Fixed Term Tenancies to new applicants, effectively giving them the means to bring to an end the notion of a 'home for life' that the Smith Institute had advocated in 2006. This legislation was then followed in 2012 by the Welfare Reform Act, in which cuts to Housing Benefit formed a central component. As George Osborne, Chancellor of the Exchequer from 2010 to 2016, made clear when he stated in his Conservative Party conference speech in 2010:

> You cannot tackle Britain's debts without tackling the unreformed welfare system … we now spend more on housing benefit than we do on the police … Ian Duncan Smith has done more than anyone in our parliament to expose the deep unfairness that traps millions of our citizens in dependency, and makes millions of others pay for it. We've been working together on the biggest reform of the welfare system since that great liberal William Beveridge.[4]

In Osborne's statement, Housing Benefit is cast as a causal agent of Britain's debts after the financial crisis. Austerity soon followed, and intensified 'epistemic violence' through scapegoating discourses that portrayed social security claimants as unworthy scroungers. Changes in the labour market structure, the greater number of women in paid work and the increase in the elderly population had caused a rising demand for welfare, while resources had become ever more restricted (Taylor-Gooby 2004). The employment restructuring that has taken place over the 40 years since 1979 has led to new patterns of employment whereby industrialised, stable and unionised jobs have given way to employment that is characterised by 'flexibility' and insecurity. As a result of these changes, the welfare state has been subject to increased pressures and faces 'a context of essentially permanent austerity' (Pierson 2002: 370).

Pierson (2002) argues that it is difficult for welfare states to embark on programmes of 'radical retrenchment' and that they remain popular and resilient in the face of economic and social changes. Nevertheless, the neoliberal advocate Milton Friedman had long held that a political crisis should never go to waste and could be used as an opportunity to implement mass change. His idea is encapsulated in the following statement, which is worth quoting at length:

> Only a crisis – actual or perceived – produces real change. When that crisis occurs, the actions that are taken depend on the ideas that are lying around. That, I believe, is our basic function: to develop alternatives to existing policies, to keep them alive and available until the politically impossible becomes the politically inevitable. (Friedman 1962/2002: xiv)

Far-reaching welfare restructuring in the UK was presented to the public as a way of making the social security system 'fairer'. The imposition of austerity enabled the ongoing transition of the welfare state into a workfare state. The French sociologist Loïc Wacquant wrote about the effects of implementing deep welfare cuts in the US, arguing that the passing of the 1996 Personal Responsibility and Work Opportunity Reconciliation Act, signed into law by President Clinton and supported by the Republican-led Congress, was enacted on the back of the demonisation of the poor, with a specific focus on single women of colour with children, referred to as 'welfare queens'. Wacquant argued that the passing of this legislation

> was never meant to fight poverty and alleviate social insecurity; on the contrary, *it was intended to normalize them*, that is to inscribe them as model experience and accepted standards of life and labor for the new service proletariat of the dualizing metropolis, a task which is indivisibly material and symbolic. (Wacquant 2009: 10)

Wacquant theorised that the ascendancy of neoliberalism since the close of the Fordist–Keynesian era would result in surging inequality, fostered by changes to wage-labour relations and the reconstruction of welfare states, which would usher in a new regime of urban marginality in first-world cities.

Austerity and the new regime of urban marginality in the UK

Following its victory in the 2015 general election, the Conservative Party enacted further legislation to extend the RTB and expand homeownership through the enactment of the Housing and Planning Act 2016. The sale of higher-value council houses was introduced to fund the extension of RTB legislation for housing association tenants. As well as this, the government's approach to affordability focused on delivering 'starter home' schemes for first-time buyers, and the expansion of the 'affordable' rent regime offered rents at up to 80% of market levels. Despite the fact that concern around housing has focused on supply and affordability, these measures point to continuing housing unaffordability for those with the lowest incomes. As Wilcock et al make clear:

> Against a background of inevitable continuing high levels of renting, no matter what the government does to boost ownership if they neglect affordability as a major issue in the rented sector they will undermine their own welfare cuts and increase the inequalities in how housing wealth is distributed. (Wilcock et al 2015: 4)

The weakening of tenure rights and the continuing loss of 'social' rents through their conversion to 'affordable' rents, coupled with Housing Benefit cuts, have undermined levels of social protection while homeownership receives increasing state support. While the Localism Act 2011 enables housing associations to implement short-term and flexible tenancies, and restricts lifetime tenancies, the Bedroom Tax works in much the same way for those already occupying the sector and who rely on rent support via Housing Benefit. These wide-ranging reforms are a political choice and will lead to greater urban marginality, as those who can pay more and who are at a lower risk of falling into rent arrears are favoured (Blessing 2016). Moreover, these policies will have the greatest impact in England, where the pattern of neoliberal housing policies is most intense.

The literature on neoliberalism cautions against viewing it as all encompassing. Rather, as Peck (2013: 139) makes clear, 'neoliberalism can only be found amongst its others, in a messy state of coexistence'.

Neoliberalism is not 'the coming of king market' (Wacquant 2013: 1), it is not anti-state (Gamble 1994) and is not about shrinking the state. In England, neoliberalisation processes can be observed in the continuing privatisation and marketisation of social housing. Since 1999 housing policy in the UK has been a matter for devolved governments (McKee et al 2017) and, as a consequence the neoliberal policies of housing reform instigated by Westminster, has faced resistance in the devolved administrations of the UK. Scotland and Wales have not followed the UK in extending the RTB; in contrast, they have abolished the policy. Further, while Housing Benefit, with the exception of Northern Ireland, remains a reserved power of the UK government, both Scotland and Northern Ireland have protected their tenants from the Bedroom Tax. This lends credence to Peck and Tickell's (2002) assertion that neoliberalism should be viewed as a variegated, uneven and contradictory process. In policy terms, England is an 'outlier' in its approach to housing vulnerable and low-income groups (McKee et al 2017).

The impact of Housing Benefit reforms on social housing providers and social landlords has resulted in a greater level of selectivity in terms of prospective tenants' financial status, as Housing Benefit funding streams are undermined by Housing Benefit cuts and direct payments to tenants under UC rules. Similarly, social landlords are much more wary of renting properties to those in receipt of Housing Benefit because of the associated financial risks around rent arrears. Blessing argues that this new selectivity

> mirrors Wacquant's 'Centaur-state', which rewards the economically established and further punishes the economically excluded. As tenants deemed to have 'income-growth potential' are repackaged for 'affordable' private rental markets, groups such as the long term unemployed, less easily 'repackaged', are feeling the impact of both quantitative and qualitative decline in the rental housing support available to them. (Blessing 2016: 168)

Wacquant argues that 'actually existing neoliberalism' involves the creation of a centaur-like state that practises laissez-faire for those at the top and transforms regimes of welfare assistance for those at the bottom into a disciplinary device to enforce low-waged work. Wacquant's work on neoliberal state-crafting is heavily focused on the US context, and it is not the intention here to suggest that we are seeing the 'Americanisation' of the UK welfare state, although the renewed emphasis on activation, work incentives and a harsher regime of sanctioning that can result in the withdrawal of benefits could be considered a form of 'Americanisation' (Alber 2010). Wacquant asserts that neoliberalism entails the re-engineering of the state rather than its wholesale dismantling. Further, his attention to how this results in advanced urban marginality is instructive for understanding the consequences of welfare state reform in the UK. Twenty years ago, Wacquant asserted that the new regimes of urban marginality in the US and the UK were aided by state retrenchment that had been pursued by their respective governments since the 1970s. For Wacquant (1999), this new marginality was fed by four specific structural circumstances that were driven forward by processes of neoliberalisation that began during the 1970s. He argues that, collectively, rising inequality, changes to wage labour (such as the rise of the gig economy), welfare state restructuring and the concentration and stigmatisation of low-income groups drive the growth in urban marginality. In the UK context the consequences of welfare state reform and the concomitant cuts to local authority budgets under the auspices of austerity are generating greater urban marginality, albeit in ways that are not immediately obvious. That is to say, the social consequences of these policies become visible only with the passage of time, through a process of deepening housing insecurity.

Throughout, this book reflects on Wacquant's (1996) features of advanced marginality. Applied to the English context, aspects of his theory are discernible in how the Bedroom Tax policy impacts on social housing tenants. The central argument here is that, collectively, the assault on Housing Benefit support and the continuing loss of social rental housing drives forward what Wacquant describes as advanced urban marginality. Its epicentre lies in rising housing inequality that does not bode well for future generations of renters faced with a dwindling supply of truly affordable housing and unable to climb onto the property ladder. In the UK, housing is a key driver of inequality and, in the English context at least, is the central mechanism through which greater marginalisation and inequality are being generated. As Wacquant (1999) has argued, in post-industrial societies welfare states do not prevent the emergence of urban marginality, and with some policies they actively generate the conditions which they claim they are trying to alleviate.

History has shown that the struggles around affordability and access to decent housing stir up tension and result in anger and discontent. History demonstrates too the failure of the PRS to accommodate low-income populations. As this chapter has shown, providing housing for those on low incomes, plus the political will to try to decently house the population and to quell rising tension, is exactly why the state intervened in the housing market in the first place. Yet, with owner-occupation out of the reach of many, we are seeing a mass return to private renting, where rents are 30% higher. As Bone (2014: 6.6) makes clear, 'the end of the "homes for life" appears as the logical counterpart to the demise of the "job for life" and the concomitant extension of "flexible" employment contracts, heralding a radically more precarious existence for growing numbers of UK citizens'. Housing precarity is becoming the norm for a growing number of low-income and vulnerable people. At its most extreme it results in 'sofa surfing', languishing in temporary accommodation or facing street homelessness. The removal of tenure rights and Housing Benefit reform coalesce as a disciplinary device which seeks to move the 'immobile' social housing tenant 'trapped in welfare dependency *by their tenure*' (Hodkinson and Robbins 2013: 69) into the low-waged precarious labour market. That is to argue that it is a two-pronged attack, with punitive housing policy working 'hand-in-glove with welfare reform' signalling 'a generational shift' (Hodkinson and Robbins 2013: 72). Hodkinson and Robbins argue that ultimately

> housing policy is being used as a strategic intervention to unblock and expand the market, complete the residualisation of social housing and draw people into an ever more economically precarious housing experience in order to boost capitalist interests. (Hodkinson and Robbins 2012: 59)

The loss of labour-based solidarities (Pilkington 2014) and the increased competition for housing that the policy creates serve to further fragment the working class, leading to inter-ethnic and intra-class tensions and divisions over the lack of affordable housing.

A note on methods and fieldwork

The Tarley estate, in which this study was conducted, lies on the outer edge of a Midlands city. The construction of the estate and the lives of the people who reside there are intricately linked to wider historical economic and social forces that have to be acknowledged in order to provide a clearer understanding and context to this study. Originally a small hamlet which lay outside of the city boundary, the neighbourhood was populated by local inhabitants, and later by munitions workers, evacuees and others who resided in the National Service hostel that was built to house workers during the Second World War. After the war it became a 'working man's' hostel providing accommodation to those flocking to the city in search of work. In the 1950s the city expanded to include Tarley within its boundary and the first 100 houses of the present-day estate were built. The damage to homes wrought by the war meant there was a massive housing need in the city and many of the hostel's occupants took up residence in Tarley when the housing estate was developed.

Tarley was the first estate in the city to be built on the 'Radburn layout'. With this layout early parts of the neighbourhood were built with the houses facing greens and footpaths, with roads and garages at the rear, with the aim of making it safer for children to play and residents to interact. Construction on the estate continued, and in 1959 a new shopping precinct was built with more than 40 shopping units. At the time the new shopping precinct was, it was said, 'the envy of many councils around the country, who came to see what a truly modern housing estate should look like' (Tarley Local History Group). Many of the houses in Tarley were built to 'Parker Morris' standards, using the 'no fines'[5] process which allowed for the quick construction of dwellings but subsequently led to problems like damp. This was an innovative period for town planning projects and the Tarley estate won a national housing award in 1960. As Tarley expanded, the city itself was experiencing a postwar 'boom' and the prospect of employment was attracting people from other parts of the country. It was, as some recall, a 'boom city' where "you could walk out of a job on Friday and walk into another one on Monday" (Jimmy).[6] A plaque on the wall of the local social club, which dates back to 1957, celebrates the history of its construction and reads:

> When the new Tarley housing estate had been erected and populated, the new residents were experiencing the usual difficulties of becoming acquainted. Miners had been brought down from Scotland to work in the local pit, families had moved from slum clearance areas and many married couples were establishing their new homes. The lack of community feeling was sensed most deeply by two men whose names will always be intertwined with the club. Both being men of initiative and foresight, they called on some 240 people who agreed to make subscriptions to the tote of 25 shillings for four years to establish the necessary fund to found the club.

The club became a central feature of the estate, with a lounge with a seating capacity of over 200 and a concert room which seats 600. The stage area was built with facilities for a 30-piece orchestra and the club also offered sporting facilities and housed an underground training gym and dressing rooms for performers. It was known as the 'Hilton of social clubs' and its size, being one of the largest social clubs in the region, attests to the working-class cultural life of the estate, the sociality and the disposable income that allowed people to partake of its facilities. The concert room accommodates a full-size boxing ring where boxing competitions are still held.

Three public houses were later built; and three churches of different religious denominations, three schools and a community centre all functioned to serve the needs of the growing population of the estate, which today stands at just under 9,000 residents. Early estate residents were said to be 'handpicked' because 'you had to have a clean rent book' (Tarley Local History Group). This was the heyday of social housing for the 'respectable' working classes. The local economy was booming and the retail businesses located on the estate felt the benefits. However, in 1963 the nearby pit closed. Manufacturing in the city was still strong but the local economy was acutely dependent on a narrow industrial base of motor vehicles and electrical and mechanical engineering. In 1971 manufacturing employment began to decline; in 1974 it accounted for 61% of total employment but the decline was such that by 1991 this had decreased to 35%. Today, only around 14% of employment in the city is in manufacturing. The loss of manufacturing was offset by only a marginal rise in service sector jobs. The result during the 1980s, an urban annual report stated, was 'unprecedented economic and social decline' in parts of the city. Unemployment rose, alongside a more worrying trend in continuous long-term unemployment. Some areas of the city suffered disproportionately from the city's dramatic economic decline and the council sought to identify 'priority' areas, defined as areas with significant concentrations of disadvantaged people, based on national indicators of social deprivation. In these areas, it was noted, the deterioration mirrored the social and economic decline of the city.

Most of the estates in the city that are defined as 'priority' neighbourhoods have high levels of social housing in comparison to other neighbourhoods. While some estates may be viewed as unpopular, the growing demand for social housing in the city means that demand outstrips supply. As such, whether estates are unpopular or not, the social housing that is still available is in high demand. The Tarley estate, like many others, while having high levels of social housing, has become a much more 'mixed tenure' estate because of the impact of RTB and because housing association new builds are often a combination of social housing, shared ownership and homes for the open market.

As the decade of the 1990s began, the urban deterioration that so concerned the council was visible in Tarley. Shops began to close and the pubs became rowdier. Money was channelled into the area, a priority estate, to provide training and resources in order to tackle the high levels of unemployment. The neighbourhood became a place where council housing was 'hard to let'. Tarley was targeted to receive funding from the Neighbourhood Renewal Fund, a government initiative set up to regenerate priority neighbourhoods. As the 1990s drew to a close the precinct, which had become almost derelict, was 'regenerated' as part of a programme involving the city council, the government housing corporation and English Partnerships, helped by private finance. The people who lived in the flats above and alongside the shops were moved out, and the homes were demolished along with the precinct. In their place, homes were built for sale on the open market and seven new shops were constructed alongside a library and Money Advice Centre.

At the time of writing, the Money Advice Centre building has closed but a reduced service is operating from the community centre. The working man's hostel, which subsequently became a homeless hostel, has closed and the land on which it stood has now been populated by mixed-tenure housing, social as well as 'affordable' homes and starter homes. The library and money advice services have both been relocated into the community centre. However, housing development on the Tarley estate still continues, with sites earmarked for the construction of new housing. During the course of this research the exteriors of many of the 'no-fines' houses and flats were re-rendered and communal areas were landscaped, vastly improving the 'look' of the neighbourhood.

Today the neighbourhood retains the social club and one pub. Of the other two pubs one was demolished and one was converted into a shop. Tarley still remains a priority estate and, given that social housing is more readily available in deprived neighbourhoods, alongside six other estates in the city it saw an increase in asylum seekers moving into the area when the city council entered into a contract with the National Asylum Support Service. This service was established in 1999 to coordinate, fund and disperse asylum seekers around the UK and relieve the pressure on housing and services in the South East of England. Ethnically, Tarley has been and remains populated by white working-class residents. In 2004 its population was 93.2% white; by 2011 this had fallen to 84.3%. There was a decline in the city's population as a whole during the 1990s. However, by 2010 population growth was the highest it had ever been and this has placed greater pressure on the social housing waiting list. Tarley, which once had a surplus of 'hard to let' properties now has high demand for social housing.

Although previous research in the neighbourhood has highlighted how some residents feel that they are stigmatised by 'postcode prejudice', it has also shown that the area benefits from a feeling of 'community spirit'. There is an active local history group which works with community members to celebrate and document the history of the estate, and a Facebook page dedicated to the estate was created as a way of countering negative images of the area.

The 31 participants who took part in this study had lived all or most of their lives in the neighbourhood. While participants have and do experience precarity in their working lives, they have had relative stability of residence, occupying their current homes for an average of 15 years. Residence within the neighbourhood was longer still, with an average length of residence within the neighbourhood of 31 years. These participants, then, comprise a relatively stable population within the neighbourhood.

Methodology

This study was conducted using ethnographic methods. Participant observation took place primarily in and around the neighbourhood. I spent time in participants' homes and in local institutions such as the social club and community centre. I attended ward forum and anti-Bedroom Tax meetings held in the local education centre, as well as protests in the city organised by the group campaigning against the Bedroom Tax. I was with participants as they realised and reacted to the threat of eviction, and helped others with the process of moving home. I accompanied people to homeless charities, Housing Benefit offices, the housing association office, court hearings and the local food bank. This method afforded me the opportunity to explore the impact of one social policy sociologically, enabling a picture of the complexity of individual lives and the *processes* through which welfare reforms, and in particular the Bedroom Tax, impacted on them in real space and time. Indeed, one of the defining features of participant observation is that it 'can give meaning to the overworked notion of *process*' (Becker 1970: 424–5; my emphasis).

Ethnography draws on a variety of methods, including participant observation, formal interviews and informal conversations, with the aim of 'gathering whatever data are available to throw light on the issues that are the emerging focus of inquiry' (Hammersly and Atkinson 2007: 3). Ethnography is often a messy business. The fieldwork for this study began in April 2013, just as the Bedroom Tax policy was being implemented. However, the research did not progress in a linear fashion, insofar as I recorded the trajectory and outcome of each and every person who was affected by the policy in the locality. Some of the interactions and informal conversations with people within the neighbourhood were not interviews in the accepted sense, as audio recording of these was neither possible nor practicable at the time. As such, some of the data included in this book is derived from anecdotal accounts provided by professionals working with people affected by the policy within the neighbourhood. Observationally, events such as 'Alfie's eviction', detailed in Chapter 4, were enabled through my contact with the anti-Bedroom Tax campaign group with whom I was in contact during the research process. Alfie's eviction was a public event that drew local media attention – his story appeared in news print and in visual form on the local news channel. In this sense the protest to prevent his eviction was a public event; however, the update on what subsequently happened to Alfie was provided anecdotally by my contact within the anti-Bedroom Tax campaign group, which was working closely with him to try to resolve his housing issues. I spoke with many people and observed many events during the course of the study but the main core of the data was derived from time spent with those who were formally interviewed. A full list of these participants is provided in the Appendix, which shows the housing outcomes of this group at last contact. The respondents chart does not detail rates of rent arrears because participants moved in and out of arrears as financial circumstances dictated. A participant might have accrued rent arrears one month but might have cleared them the following month, only to accrue them again at a later date. For this reason an accurate picture of the rates of arrears was difficult to track. Formal interviews often took place in the presence of other family members and friends, and while they too gave their consent to participate, for the purposes of clarity I have recorded only the names of the householders.

Interviews

A snowball sampling technique was used to recruit the participants in this study. Initial participants were asked if they knew other people who were subject to the Bedroom Tax, and in this way more interviews were generated. Interview participants were also recruited via participant observation in neighbourhood institutions, where a conversation would lead to participation. A sample of 31 participants was generated and interviews were audio-recorded and transcribed. The sample was purposive in that it sought participants who were, or who had been, subject to paying the Bedroom Tax and who resided within the neighbourhood of Tarley. It thus did not seek, or produce, a statistically representative sample but, rather, in line with much ethnographic research, aimed 'to target the people who have the knowledge desired and who may be willing to divulge it to the ethnographer' (Hammersly and Atkinson 2007: 106).

I employed semi-structured biographical interviewing, with the interview schedule divided into themes pertaining to participants' early lives on the estate, social housing histories, employment status, social relationships, neighbourhood perceptions, social housing perceptions, leisure, debt, Bedroom Tax and welfare questions. These questions aimed to uncover a participant's past and present experiences, together with their attitudes and feelings, rather than to simply establish their material situation and how it had been affected by the policy reform. In order to understand the effect of possible displacement and to give a clearer picture of the ways in which lives were lived before and after the introduction of this policy it was important to uncover feelings and emotions. Semi-structured interviewing allowed for flexibility, which was important, as during the course of conducting this research it became clear that for some participants the past was a painful place to revisit. Of the 31 participants, 22 were female and 9 male. The sample is thus gender skewed. The respondent set also includes mainly older people: the average age of participants was 48 years. This is due to the fact that the Bedroom Tax, by its very nature, tends to affect an older cohort whose children have grown up and left the family home.

Additional interviews were also conducted with key professionals who worked with or were in contact with people subject to the Bedroom Tax. I interviewed a housing officer who worked for the largest social housing provider in Tarley, the local vicar who helped to organise the local food bank, a solicitor from the law centre, a local doctor, a member of staff from the local Money Advice Centre and a member of the city-wide anti-Bedroom Tax campaign. The aim of these interviews was to shed light on how this policy was impacting at the neighbourhood level and to allow for cross-referencing between personal and professional experiences.

3

Living in a state of insecurity

In order to understand the impact that paying the extra charge for the Bedroom Tax made on the lives of the tenants in this study, the scene must be set by outlining how participants managed financially prior to its introduction. Of the 31 participants, 11 were claiming DLA for a range of physical and mental disabilities. One participant was going through the process of being moved from DLA onto the new benefit which is in the process of replacing this, known as the Personal Independence Payment (PIP). Eight participants were claiming Employment and Support Allowance (ESA) and one of these had failed the ESA work capability test and was, at the time of interview, waiting for his appeal to be heard in court. In the meantime his benefit had been reduced to the level of Job Seeker's Allowance (JSA), meaning he would be sanctioned if he could not provide evidence that he was actively looking for work. Three participants were caring for a household member who had a disability and four of the participants were in employment, all part time, one with a seven-hours-per-week contract. One participant was a full-time university student and the remaining four participants were unemployed.

Persistent poverty: insecure starting points

A 2014 report by the Council of Europe's Committee on Social Rights stated that the current level of the UK's benefits, including incapacity benefits and JSA was 'manifestly inadequate' (ECSR: 2014: 18). When the reduction in Housing Benefit, as a consequence of the Bedroom Tax, is factored in, the amount a tenant has to live on is further reduced, as they have to make up the shortfall in rent. For those who are under-occupying by one bedroom the amount for which they are liable is around £14 per week, rising to £24 per week if the tenant/s have two spare rooms or more. Respondents' narratives tell stories of 'getting by' and 'plodding along'; indeed this was a recurrent rather than recent feature of their biographies. Many had cycled in and out of low-paid, precarious employment and had fallen back on the social security system when work was in short supply.

Mary, aged 59, moved into a two-bedroom council house property in Tarley with her friend at the age of 19 after leaving an unmarried mothers' home with her baby daughter. Mary's friend had a child too and they shared the cost of the rent between them. Mary had spent much of her life living in care homes and found it difficult to manage financially as a young lone parent. She talked pragmatically about how she got by:

> 'I got into crime I'm afraid and so around Tar Road I had a gas meter, coin meters and err, so I used to break into them for money, and they found out. I mean I had my gas cut off, I only had Jane at the time, my daughter. I mean she had no gas, so I had no means of cooking, the welfare, it was called the welfare then, they lent me a little Baby Belling cooker, but that didn't work, that only worked for a while, and so they wouldn't replace it. To cook I used to have a little camping stove, a little Calor gas, gas bottle, and a new little Breville thing and that's how I used to cook me meals. And a coal fire, cus if I run out of gas bottles I had nothing to cook on, so I used to have to like do egg on toast on the coal fire (laughs). You improvised when you had to, I improvised (laughs) you'd get black bits in the fried egg but that was just a bit of the coal or something spitting out (laughing). I managed, you managed ...' (Mary)

Mary described herself as of mixed ethnicity and her child was black. She moved into a predominantly white neighbourhood in an era when attitudes towards people of colour were overtly racist. Additionally, in 1970s Britain unmarried mothers faced financial and social disadvantage in comparison to two-parent families, with poverty particularly affecting the children of lone mothers. Managing was Mary's priority, and with no family to support her she tried to get by in any way she could to bring up her child, to heat her home and feed herself and her daughter. Mary reminisced about the state of the maisonette she occupied:

> 'Two-bedroom maisonette, an' erm, no central heating. There was just a gas fire, there was nothing, I mean it was, it was an old-fashioned kitchen, no cupboards. I mean I had one of those French dresser things but not a dresser as you think, no new ones like with the glass doors on. I mean they were awful, that was the only cupboards there, like, and a Belfast sink, even though they're coming in, like,

they weren't very what's a name then and I was overrun
with mice.' (Mary)

Mary lived for ten years in the maisonette, eventually moving into
a three-bedroom house around the corner from where she lived,
remaining within the neighbourhood. The fact that Mary had one
child and was relocating to a three-bedroom property mattered little
to the local council, who at that time were responsible for the social
housing stock in the city. The house she moved into was of the 'no
fines' construction. It did not have central heating and Mary said that
the property was "difficult to let". In subsequent years, Mary gave
birth to a son and remained in the property after both her children had
grown up and left home. Mary, like all of the participants in this study,
had spent her life fluctuating between periods of low-skilled work
and benefit claims over many years. While precarious employment
appears to be the defining condition of contemporary working life,
the working biographies of those in this study highlight that this was
a normal feature of their lives. The nature of the work they did,
particularly the women, was low paid and insecure, but what mattered
most was the availability of work rather than its security.

Since the financial crash and the Great Recession finding work had
become increasingly difficult for participants. For example, Jane, a
service assistant in a supermarket, working on a seven-hours-per-week
contract, told me that she had never understood the word 'recession'
until it took her over two years to find a job. For many, taking out
loans from doorstep loan companies such as Mutual and Provident
provided the only means by which to fund Christmas presents and
white goods. That's the thing about experiencing poverty: having to
replace a fridge or cooker that is broken can be a financial shock that
can lead to debt. There is no rainy day fund, no savings account, no
money in reserve to replace broken household goods. The point here
is that participants struggled to get by *before* the Bedroom Tax policy
was introduced. So when the Bedroom Tax was implemented the extra
cost involved in the under-occupancy charge represented a significant
potential loss of income for participants who were just about managing
to get by. And it left them wondering how they would find the money
to pay. The Bedroom Tax was introduced into lives that were *already*
financially insecure and precarious. The stripping away of economic
opportunity and inadequate social provision led to the accumulation
of hardship. Participants did their best to budget on low incomes and
benefits, but persistent poverty left them in a vulnerable position when
confronted with further economic shocks.

Enter the 'Bedroom Tax'

In the neighbourhood of Tarley, the majority of the stock of council housing was transferred to the RSL, Media Housing Association, in 2000 after tenants voted in favour of stock transfer in a city-wide ballot. Alongside Media, a number of other social landlords have sprung up in the area and built homes, but Media remain in control of the majority of the stock. Ahead of the implementation of the Bedroom Tax in April 2013, they produced a DVD and sent this out alongside letters to their tenants in order to inform them about what the policy was and how it would affect their rent payments. Housing association officers were also sent out to visit people to discuss the forthcoming reductions in Housing Benefit. Nevertheless, it was clear that some of the participants in this study, particularly those who were tenants of smaller housing associations, were confused about the policy and felt they had not been given enough information. Of the 31 participants, four had initiated steps to downsize prior to the policy's coming into effect. Others, while acknowledging that they had been aware of the Bedroom Tax, and had heard talk and speculation about it, felt that they would not be affected by it. Louise, a part-time worker, articulates this false assumption:

Louise:	I heard it as gossip … erm, I can't even remember where, but I heard it as gossip and I didn't think it would affect me at all.
Interviewer:	Because you were working?
Louise:	Yeah, erm, and not only that everyone had a room and so I didn't think it would affect me at all, because I thought well every room is occupied … and why would I be affected … I thought do you know, people on benefits might be affected, people on a lower benefit than me, people not working, and I thought it was just out of order that people would do that, and I still don't understand the whole Bedroom Tax, it's, it's not empty, somebody's sleeping in it. Somebody's sleeping in it, it's being used, it's got a body and a bed, so why am I being charged for a bedroom? It's being used! (Louise)

Louise had three daughters who lived with her in a four-bedroom property. The policy affected her because of the age restrictions on sharing a room, meaning that her daughters were not entitled to their own rooms. The same restrictions applied to Cath, who lived in a four-bedroom property with her four children, two of whom, because of their ages and gender, should have been sharing. At this early stage of the policy's implementation many said they were confused as to how it would affect them. Because of this confusion, some of the participants fell into rent arrears without even knowing, as the following interview excerpt from 55-year-old Jimmy highlights:

Interviewer: So when did you first hear about it?
Jimmy: Erm, I got a letter off the council, Media HA, saying we're putting a Bedroom Tax on this flat, but it never stated when it was gonna start or nothing like that or how you're supposed to pay it, or how much I was supposed to pay.
Interviewer: Did anyone come out and see you?
Jimmy: No.
Interviewer: Did you go up and see them?
Jimmy: I think I got another letter then … stating that they wanted me to pay for the extra room, I think it come to thirteen pound seventy pence, but I had nothing to say where I had to pay it, or no card or anything like that, where to pay it, nothing like that, so next minute I got, I got a bill in for over four hundred pound … so I went up to that council office (HA office) up there, Media, and I seen the girl and I said can you tell me what I'm supposed to do about this, this bedroom tax, and she said, got on her computer and all that like, I wouldn't worry about it Jimmy, cus it's not that much money. Four hundred pound, I said, what do you mean? She said well you've still got your month's rent to come off that, three hundred and odd pound like, you know, what the council pay. I said that's all right, so I agreed then, I was still in arrears, I agreed with her then, I think it was nearly fourteen pound a week and I agreed then. I said look love, how do I pay it? She said well you can come into the office and pay it, or we can send you a card out and pay it at the post office. I said well that will do me, send me a card out and I will pay it every week at the post office. So I waited and waited and

waited, this went on for eight weeks before I got a card to pay me rent. I had eight weeks' arrears again because of the stupid girl in the office who sent the card out. And then I got a phone call off a bloke, I think it was from that office up there, Media, saying I'm phoning up about the arrears over your rent. I said listen mate I've been waiting forever, I'm telling ya now I'm not gonna lose me rag, I'm gonna tell ya once then I'm putting this phone down. I said I was in your office eight weeks ago, I seen a girl I told her I was gonna pay twenty pound a week as soon as you lot send me a card to start paying it … He said you know you should of come into the office and started paying it straight away. I said why do I have to put myself out, come all the way to the office to pay money to you'se when you haven't got the decency to send me a card out straight away. And I told him, I explained to him about my health condition and all that like, I was diagnosed with cancer two year ago, and I said I can't get around very well mate, do you think I can run up to that office every week, I said. At least my house is near the shops, five minutes' walk, I said. I'm not running up to your office every week paying you twenty pound, I said, I've got the card now and I'll pay the twenty pound that I said I would pay till my arrears is paid off and then I'll pay the right amount.

Some participants misunderstood the Bedroom Tax to be a Media Housing Association policy rather than an initiative imposed by central government. As such, they assumed that if they were not living in a Media property they would be exempt. Others, particularly those tenants who struggled with literacy issues and mental health difficulties, appeared even more confused. Billy, for example, thought that the policy would come into effect in September 2013, five months after its actual introduction in April 2013:

'But this is the thing, not everyone, that's the point, it started in London in April, some people like our friends, Shaz who lives next door to us, is the same, hers don't start till the first week in September and other people have told us that it's September. We don't know if it's to do with your initials or anything like that but some are paying it now and some are not paying it till September.' (Billy)

There appeared then to be no systematic and comprehensive strategy for preparing tenants. Rather, housing associations initiated their own strategies to prepare and inform tenants, some being more successful than others. One of the smaller housing associations was located in another city, which made it difficult to speak with a housing officer in person. Added to this was the confusion created by speculation and gossip about what actually constituted a bedroom – a factor that was fuelled by speculation about the policy and bedroom size in the media. When talking to people in the community, in the smoking area of the social club or in the community centre, the talk was often about this 'new Bedroom Tax'. Some participants had heard that if a room was below a certain size then the Bedroom Tax did not apply. This often led to people thinking they did not have to pay. Others struggled to afford to pay. These factors, taken together, resulted in a significant number of participants falling quickly into rent arrears. This was the case particularly for older single participants living in three-bedroom properties and paying the maximum of £24 per week. Bob, for example, quickly fell into arrears because he had also seen a reduction in his weekly benefit due to being found 'fit for work' after attending a Work Capability Assessment (WCA). This assessment takes place in order to assess or reassess an individual's entitlement to ESA. Bob was managing on £71 per week, out of which he was then liable to pay £24 for two spare bedrooms.

For those who had previous rent arrears, the situation became even more difficult. Previous rent arrears, participants stated, were almost always caused by a change in circumstances. For example, if a partner or child left the property a new claim had to be made to the Benefit Office and delays in processing new claims often resulted in rent arrears. In these cases, and when tenants found it difficult to pay, rent arrears very quickly reached levels where the housing association sought possession orders through the county court. This was the case with Marlene and Eric, who had accrued rent arrears prior to the introduction of the policy but were paying them back at a small weekly rate which they could afford. Others, like Jessica (who had no pre-existing arrears), had accumulated arrears of over £400 because she could afford to make only incremental payments on the shortfall of £24 per week. Jessica soon began receiving letters warning her that repossession proceedings would commence if the arrears were not paid.

Once tenants were in rent arrears their housing association would send out a letter of 'Notice Seeking Possession', informing them that failure to pay could result in a possession order being made and that they were at risk of losing their home. These letters in particular caused great anxiety, and this anxiety was compounded by the fact that unless arrears were cleared there was little chance that the tenant would be allowed to downsize or swap properties because of housing association rules prohibiting tenants from moving with outstanding arrears. High levels of insecurity and anxiety have been shown to impact negatively on those whose health is already compromised by illness and disease. The widespread confusion about the policy and the pressure to find extra money to pay the shortfall in Housing Benefit, coupled with rising rent arrears, destabilised participants. The security afforded by Housing Benefit, guaranteeing housing security as it did amid the spectre of precarious employment and ill-health, had been undermined with the implementation of the policy. Their housing security was one of the few things that they had been able to rely upon. For participants with caring responsibilities and for those who were dealing with physical and mental health issues, the fear that they could potentially lose their home became a constant source of anxiety.

Impact on physical and mental health

The Bedroom Tax particularly affects those who have ongoing health and disability problems. This is not surprising, given that nearly two-thirds of those affected nationally have a disability (DWP 2012). This was made clear by a number of reports (McCafferty 2012) showing that a high percentage of sick and disabled people would be liable to pay and, as a result, would have either to move or to absorb the reduction in Housing Benefit, as they were deemed unfit for work by doctors and government medical assessment agencies. In this respect, the Bedroom Tax has little utility as a way to 'incentivise' work. Nineteen of the participants in this study were claiming either ESA or DLA, indicating that they had a physical or mental health issue that acted as a barrier to employment.

Work capability tests, introduced under New Labour, are designed to encourage and support claimants of sickness and disability benefits back into the workplace. This is achieved by sorting claimants into two distinct groups: the Support Group, for those unable to work; and the Work Related Activity Group (WRAG), for those deemed capable of doing some work. Those assessed as 'fit for work' are moved onto JSA and their benefit is cut to a lower rate. The testing procedure has been highly controversial, as disability campaigners highlight a number of deaths among people who have been found 'fit for work'. Analysis of the WCA and ESA system between January and August 2011 showed that 1,100 claimants died after being placed in the ESA WRAG, and a further 1,600 people died before their assessment had been completed. Moreover, the report highlights that the medical profession, voluntary associations, charities and individuals share concerns about the WCA. According to the British Medical Association in 2012, the WCA was 'not fit for purpose' (We Are Spartacus 2012: 67).

Under the new regime of welfare restructuring in the UK the sick and disabled are being drawn into the category of 'undeserving' poor, a shift from being seen historically as a 'deserving' group. As Hancock and Mooney (2012: 3) make clear, the sick and disabled 'have emerged as a relatively new "scrounger" population'. DLA, a non-means-tested benefit, which was in the process of being changed to PIP and subject to assessment, is increasingly being seen as an out-of-work benefit (Wood and Grant 2010). Katie had a range of physical health problems. She had undergone an operation on her brain in 2009 and had additional spinal problems. At the time of interview she was going through the process of being moved onto the new PIP system, as she explained:

> 'I've put in a claim for that PIP, that Personal Independence Payment, erm, I still haven't heard back from em yet. I had a home visit, cus I asked for a home visit erm … to come out on 23 December and I'm still waiting. I phoned them last week and they said there's been that much of a backlog that they've had to bring extra workers in so they're trying to do the best to get it sorted. But I'm still waiting. This month alone, just from January I've been four times already [hospital], and we ain't even at the end of the month yet. So you tell me who pays them bus fares and do you know what I mean? It's not just bus fares, you have to buy yourself a cup of tea when you're there cus sometimes I'm there for hours cus I have to have MRI scans all the time, X-rays all the time. I'm there all the time, then they say I'm not entitled to this disability money.' (Katie)

Many of the participants in this study were being impacted on by the overhaul of the social security system initiated under the Welfare Reform Act 2012, so the Bedroom Tax represented 'one hit among many' (Bragg et al 2015: 78–9). However, the Bedroom Tax policy had distinct impacts, particularly when people were struggling to pay, and arrears began to mount up. Participants had dealt with financial insecurity – it was an abiding feature of their lives – but the threat of losing a property they called home, repossession orders and potential eviction caused serious psychological stress, or what Bragg et al (2015: 82) describe as 'insecurity and psychological homelessness'. The situation was made worse by tenants feeling that they had nowhere to turn to for help, as the following field diary extract details.

FIELD DIARY
22 February 2014

I go around to Rory's flat to do the interview; I'm a bit apprehensive and not really sure that he's up to it. He has not long come out of hospital after having surgery for throat or mouth cancer, and it appears as if some of his lower jaw has been removed. When I saw him at the weekend he assured me he was fine to talk to me, and he gave me his address and phone number and we arranged a day to do the interview. Because of the cancer, it's quite difficult to understand what Rory is saying at times. When I pull up in my car outside his block I start getting a bit apprehensive, and decide to play things by ear. Rory lives in a two-bedroom flat on the third floor of a block of flats. He's expecting me, so buzzes me up straight away when I press the buzzer. He meets me at the door, and we go in and sit down. He offers me tea, and I begin by asking Rory about his health. He says he's OK. 'I'm just worried about this Bedroom Tax', he says, 'I've heard that some people shouldn't be paying it, do you know about that?' He then explains how he's lived there for 15 years and doesn't want to move, but that he's finding it difficult to cope financially. At this point I decide I'm not going to follow through with the interview because I get the distinct impression that Rory just wants some help and advice, and he doesn't look well. Rory is 55 years old, he's tall and he looks like he was a well-built man until illness took its toll, his clothes look too big for him. I explain that he's not eligible for exemption (this exempts people who have lived in their properties for 16 years and have been claiming housing benefit continuously) under the Bedroom Tax loophole, but that he should apply for the Discretionary Housing Payment. He says he hasn't so far because he doesn't want to phone them because of his speech impediment. I tell him I will get him a form and bring it round and help him fill it out if needs be.

The psychological and emotional pressure that housing precarity generated in turn had an impact on tenants' physical wellbeing. Wilkinson (1996) argues that psychosocial stress is detrimental to health, showing that health deteriorates as a consequence of unemployment, mediated by insecurity about income, autonomy and identity. He states that 'housing insecurity, whether caused by council plans or difficulty in keeping up with rent or mortgage payments, has much in common with fears of unemployment' (Wilkinson 1996: 178). The psychosocial stress experienced by tenants who cannot work is related to their fears about maintaining a home rather than fears about unemployment. Many had experienced periods of economic inactivity, but this experience paled in comparison to the potential of losing the one constant in their lives: a secure social housing tenancy. The sense of anger, desperation and worry that was evident in participants' narratives suggests that the Bedroom Tax led to a feeling of housing insecurity. Moreover, the stress was prolonged over time and became an ongoing worry as tenants struggled to keep up weekly rent payments. Such prolonged stress 'is often all it takes to damage health' (Wilkinson 1996: 184). Socioeconomic disadvantage affects health through psychosocial pathways. Germane to these cases, the threat and insecurity generated by the prospect of losing a tenancy matters because what it means to have a secure home is emotionally charged and fosters in people a sense of ontological security. Kinnvall (2004: 747) argues that 'ontological security is maintained when home is able to provide a site of constancy in the social and material environment'. When the home as a bearer of security is undermined, ontological fear is the outcome. Rather than providing a source of security, the home became for participants the source of their feelings of vulnerability. They felt that they were being 'forced' from their homes, and made material sacrifices in their lives in an attempt to safeguard their housing security.

For those with mental health problems, in particular, the Bedroom Tax was managed sometimes through a strategy of total avoidance. However, avoiding letters and correspondence from the housing association and courts resulted eventually in eviction. The local vicar recounted how this had happened to one of her parishioners, and I also spoke informally with Darren, who suffered from mental health problems. He was woken one morning by housing officials and locksmiths who had come to evict him. He spoke honestly about how he had quickly fallen into arrears and was then unable to face opening any letters he received: "it's my own fault; I just buried my head in the sand". He subsequently stayed with his sister, sleeping on her couch until he found private rented accommodation in the area.

Matters were not helped by the widespread confusion among tenants about how the Bedroom Tax applied to them, a situation compounded by the stripping away of local support services. The local library had hosted an outreach service run by the Housing Benefit Office where claimants could discuss Housing Benefit issues with an adviser. This service had been disbanded, due to cutbacks. The Housing Benefit Office in the city centre had also disbanded the service whereby tenants could walk in and wait to speak to an adviser. Instead, an appointment had to be made by phoning the office. However, getting through to the office often took time and tenants would be placed on hold, using up their phone credit. The perceived lack of help served to increase the stress and worry, as Jessica made clear:

> 'I ain't gotta clue, no one's helped me, I've tried to phone I've tried to. I've gone up there [Money Advice Centre] I've gone to the one in town, tried everyone, the Money Advice, the library even like, they're just like … I'm thinking oh my God, no one … they're trying to get you out the house but no one's helping me!' (Jessica)

Participants very often became visibly distressed when recounting their experience. During interviews some participants broke down in tears when they spoke about receiving what they perceived as threatening letters about their arrears and the threat of court action. Others said the strain had caused deterioration of existing health problems and weight loss. Further, it caused greater isolation, as participants said that a game of bingo or going to the club for a drink was no longer possible because they could not afford the expense. June, a cancer sufferer who also suffers epilepsy, explained how her health has suffered:

> 'Yeah causes me to have more fits, my epilepsy pills have been put up. I was up the hospital two weeks ago in fact and they gave me more tablets cus I explained to them about it, I was that stressed, I was that stressed thinking what if I can't afford to pay it … I've lost weight, look; look at how much weight I've lost. Ruby [June's friend], she's gotta pay on her house, she's normally about somewhere. It's causing an awful lot of people to go to the doctor's and all that. Ruby she, she's a nervous wreck and she don't go out anymore.' (June)

Tenants felt that they now had little control or autonomy over their housing situation, which left them feeling scared. This fear was oppressive; it preoccupied them, impacting on their health and social relationships. Social housing tenants may have lived precarious lives before the introduction of the Bedroom Tax, but they did not have to worry about their ability to maintain a housing tenancy, because Housing Benefit covered all of their rent. The introduction of the Bedroom Tax represented a new insecurity that had adverse impacts on the health and wellbeing of tenants already compromised either physically or mentally. This corresponds to the findings of Moffatt et al (2015), who, in their qualitative study of the effects of the Bedroom Tax, concluded that the policy increased poverty and debt. This impacted negatively on respondents' mental health and social relationships 'and their ability to carry out normal social roles' (Moffatt et al 2015: 1). Their study, like this one, challenges the government's own impact assessment of the policy, since it refutes the claim that the Bedroom Tax would have no impact on health and wellbeing. Indeed, in contrast to this initial report, the government's own evaluation of the policy (Clarke et al 2015) has likewise shown it to have a detrimental effect on the emotional wellbeing of tenants, alongside rising food poverty.

The impact on health and wellbeing has had a knock-on effect on general practitioners (GPs), who have seen a rise in their workload. More than two-thirds (68%) of GPs say that the reduction in benefits has had a harmful impact on their patients' health (Iacobucci 2014). Both the local doctor and the vicar in Tarley noted that people who were dealing with welfare reform changes, be it Bedroom Tax, sanctions or WCAs, were presenting with greater levels of stress and anxiety. This was manifest in the barely contained despair, embarrassed tears and a pervasive sense of futility among participants who felt that they were on the verge of losing their homes. In the next section I describe in greater detail the extent of food poverty among participants and the everyday difficulties they faced in managing household bills. Food poverty was prevalent among participants in this study, and the inability to meet adequate dietary and nutritional needs can be particularly detrimental to those whose immune systems are already compromised by disease.

'This new poverty'

Payment of the Bedroom Tax could be sporadic, particularly for those tenants who had children. An unexpected expense such as a birthday, a child needing new shoes or a dressing-up costume for World Book Day could disrupt the budget. Indeed, parents sought to shield their children from the effects of financial hardship by maintaining their inclusion in school and other activities, even if this meant getting into rent arrears. In this way, parents attempted to protect their children from the 'universal and immutable link between poverty and shame' (Walker 2014: 1). In the context of poverty, shame or even the threat of shame can have negative consequences as individuals risk indebtedness as they try to behave 'as normal' (Walker 2014: 52).

The food bill was often the only flexible household outgoing and thus was frequently the first thing to be cut back. Indeed, studies have highlighted the high prevalence of food poverty among those liable for the Bedroom Tax (Bragg et al 2015; Clarke et al 2015). Riches, writing in 1997, observed how 'when food expenditures have to be weighed against the increasing price of rent, utilities, clothing and other essentials it is the food bill which invariably suffers' (Riches 1997: 169). Within families there may be a hierarchy of food needs. In this study, parents and grandparents often went without food in order that other family members were not deprived: June stated that she often missed meals to provide food for her grandchildren, whom she regularly cared for. Cath tried to shop economically, but explained how her children made distinctions between cheaper brands:

> 'You just can't afford to live, ten pound electric, straight away, toiletries, trying to put decent food in the cupboards, the kids these days when you're trying to give them a cheap tin of beans, and they're like "I ain't eating that". I mean, things have upgraded but you ain't got the money to upgrade with it, like literally its bad.' (Cath)

Others, because of health problems, shopped locally for food, which cost more than shopping in supermarkets. Participants could tell me the price of a loaf of bread or tin of soup and expressed anger at the rising cost of food and the government's apparent ignorance about the cost of living. Jane, for example, referred to an instance when the former Prime Minister was asked how much a loaf of bread cost: "when I heard that bloke asking him how much the bread was, he didn't know, David Cameron … well that's just wrong!" Others such as Eric and Mo showed resistance to the policy. Eric, a lone parent with two children, had been forced to use the local food bank after his benefits had been sanctioned by the DWP and he fell deeper into rent arrears. He spoke about how grateful he was that the food bank had come to his aid at a time of crisis, but also mentioned that at the food bank you have to take what you are given, which meant that he often had to serve his children food they did not like. Eric decided that feeding his children would take priority over paying the Bedroom Tax, as he explained: "I'd get stressed out and that, worried and that … I thought the more I pay to you the less food goes in my kids' mouths, what option do I have, I ain't paying you …" However, by choosing to prioritise the needs of his children over his rent he ultimately found himself in a situation where he had to abandon his tenancy before the bailiffs came to evict him for rent arrears. Katie's daughter, Ellen, summed their situation up thus: "it was either pay the debt and go without food or have food and not pay the debt, that's how it was basically … it was a nightmare …". Mo had been paying the Bedroom Tax by direct debit. She and her son had been living without a cooker after it was condemned by the gas inspector. After a particularly bad week, and having no food in the cupboards, she decided to take the Bedroom Tax money out of the cash machine before it was debited to the housing association. Mo knew this would put her into rent arrears but at that point she did not care. She bought food and a deep-fat fryer with the money so she could cook a hot meal.

Three of the participants in this study had resorted to using the local food bank. They spoke about their embarrassment at having to go and ask for donated food. In order to receive a food parcel an individual has to explain why they are eligible before receiving a voucher from a provider. Food bank vouchers were provided by a number of agencies within the community but the main outlet had become the vicarage, which helped to organise the food bank in Tarley. The local Money Advice Centre had stopped issuing vouchers to people whom they were not actively working with. The vicar explained this policy as follows:

> 'They do give them, but only to clients that they're working with on other issues. So if they have an appointment with a client over, say, filling in benefits forms they'll give a voucher to them, but you can't just walk in the front door and ask for a voucher because they found they were getting so many people doing that and potentially a bit of abuse sometimes.' (Local vicar)

Having to ask for a food voucher was a stressful experience in itself. Bob had heard that he could obtain a food bank voucher from his doctor. Bob suffered from mental health problems. He was trying to maintain his Bedroom Tax payments but this was, he said, leaving him with a "pittance" to live on. He approached his doctor for a food bank voucher, but after the doctor explained that they did not distribute vouchers Bob became angry and upset and the doctor threatened to call in the receptionist if he did not calm down. Bob explained how he had found the encounter humiliating and was at his "wits' end", "I don't know whether I'm coming or going", he said. Writing about the experience of food bank use in the UK, Kayleigh Garthwaite made clear how:

> The hundreds of people I met did not want to come to the food bank. It was not something they planned to do because they didn't fancy going to Tesco for their food shopping. It was a last resort, a tipping point into a whole new realm of indignity. (Garthwaite 2016: 149–50)

Having to use the food bank represented a new, more acute level of poverty that participants tried to avoid because of the stigma associated with it, although they recognised that there might come a time when they had no other option. The rise in food poverty in the UK and the concomitant rise in food bank use has been attributed to cuts to the social security system and rising in-work poverty. Participants admitted that getting by was 'a struggle', but for many there was always someone else worse off: those that could not rely on the support of family or friends, those with addiction problems and those having to use a food bank or having to live in the local homeless hostel, which was perceived as housing the truly 'down and outs'. Participants said they were 'surviving', and felt they were 'in the same boat' as others in the neighbourhood. Poverty was viewed in relational terms; it helped to compare oneself to others who appeared to be in a worse financial situation. However, some respondents felt that they had sunk to a new level of poverty, what one participant described as "this new poverty" (Mo), because of the Bedroom Tax. Being faced with losing one's home left tenants feeling demoralised and despairing:

Interviewer: In comparison to other people around here, would you say you were richer, poorer, the same?
Jess: Poorer.
Interviewer: Do you feel poor?
Jess: Yeah, I do. I've given up on me house cus they want me out, what's the point in doing anything now …

Life on a low income was mitigated through acts of reciprocity such as borrowing money, milk, bread or sugar from a neighbour, family or friends. Borrowing a 'tenner' from someone was normal, because next week you might be in the same situation. There was no ethos of 'never a lender or a borrower be', because they knew that they might be in the same position next week, and if they did not pay back then they would not be entitled to ask again. Such are the rules. It was how people got by; "swings and roundabouts" as one participant put it. The reform of the welfare system and the cut to Housing Benefit was seen as leaving individuals with a wholly inadequate income. Participants did not imply that benefit payments were too low, but that the state, in cutting Housing Benefit, could no longer guard against homelessness, the ultimate marker of poverty as Ruby explained:

> 'Gutted and scared, terrified to think that one day they could … if I didn't keep up the payments that they could come round one day, "right you've gotta get out", change the locks so I couldn't get back in, couldn't get none of my possessions. They don't care about that but she [housing officer] said "at the end of the day it's my job to do it". Must be a heartless cow. That's what they're doing to people though, if you don't pay it they'll just come round and change your locks, they don't care where you live, they don't care if you've got kids. Especially with Christmas coming up, it comes so quick, bills going up, its, it's just a snowball, its mental. I said to Jay I feel like getting a petrol bomb and blowing the place up then they'll have to rehouse me somewhere cheaper … sometimes I feel like doing it, they'd probably put me in a fucking hostel or summat … (voice rises) that's how, sometimes that's how I feel.' (Ruby)

A Bedroom Tax payment would often be missed when a utility bill needed to be paid. While participants intended to make up the payment at a later date, many struggled to do so. Those who were in rent arrears tried to clear them by paying extra rent on top of what they were already paying, but in most cases this meant that the Bedroom Tax effectively rose because of the arrears payment. Paying in this way, rather than in one lump sum, prolonged the period that a tenant was in arrears. As will be shown in Chapter 4, this situation had repercussions insofar as it affected participants' eligibility to downsize to smaller accommodation.

Reducing levels of benefits is seen as a way to activate labour market participation, and one of the central aims of reducing Housing Benefit for under-occupiers is to incentivise tenants to find work or to increase their working hours (DWP 2010b). But the Bedroom Tax has done nothing more than compound the health issues that a high proportion of participants were experiencing. As Wacquant (1999: 1643) asserts, 'states do make a difference ... as *generative* as well as *remedial* institutions'. And this policy is generating deeper poverty and having a detrimental impact on wellbeing. As the remedial functions of the state are being diminished, charitable organisations are having to pick up the pieces. Food banks are being left to rescue those who have fallen through the social security safety net. Their use has risen, with 20,247,042 meals given to people in food poverty in 2013–14, a 54% increase on 2012–13 (Cooper et al 2014). This widespread food poverty has been attributed directly to cuts in welfare provision (Cooper et al 2014; Garthwaite 2016). In a lecture about his book *First World Hunger Revisited* (Riches and Silvasti 2014), Graham Riches talked about food banks providing 'wasted food for surplus people' – that is, people who are surplus to the requirements of the labour market. Dowler (2014: 160) argues that in terms of food poverty 'an astonishing and scarcely imaginable situation' is unfolding in the UK which is exacerbated by the 'systematic dismantling of the postwar consensus on the need for and maintenance of a welfare state' (Dowler 2014: 164). Reducing welfare support in order to enforce low-wage dependency may be central to the ideology of neoliberalism (Peck 2001; Harvey 2005) but, rather than incentivising work and reducing so-called 'welfare dependency', the reduction in Housing Benefit has abetted the onset of deepening food poverty.

Reproducing insecurity

The Bedroom Tax affected all working-age tenants in social housing who were claiming Housing Benefit and who were classed as under-occupying. Single parents who were working part time were liable to pay, as their income from employment was insufficient to cover all of their housing costs. Thirteen of the participants in this study had dependants living with them. Four of these parents had either mental or physical health problems and were claiming some form of Housing Benefit because they were on a low income; therefore their children were living in a low-income household. This study did not seek to capture the voices or experiences of many of the children who lived with research participants. However, as the research progressed it became apparent that they were being affected by the policy. Older teenage children, such as Katie's daughter, Ellen, were present during interviews and freely expressed their views. The children of participants were not immune to the worry and anxiety that affected their parents. Indeed studies that have analysed the subjective experience of child poverty from children's own accounts show that 'low-income children have a keen understanding of how poverty impacts on their lives and the social and material uncertainty that low income brings' (Ridge 2011: 75). A study exploring the impact of the Bedroom Tax on children and their education (Bragg et al 2015) documented how school staff and parents were concerned that children were indirectly distressed by their parents' hunger, exhaustion, depression and sadness as a result of the Bedroom Tax.

The parents in this study did not explicitly explain to their children that they were paying the Bedroom Tax. Older children, however, seemingly became aware as the stress on a parent increased. Katie's daughter, Ellen, aged 18, helped to take care of her mother, who was suffering a host of physical ailments that restricted her mobility. Katie eventually downsized to a flat when paying the Bedroom Tax became untenable and she had to resort to using the food bank. However, because of Katie's mobility problems it was Ellen who had to go and ask for the voucher and attend the food bank:

Interviewer:	How did it make you feel having to use the food bank?
Ellen:	Embarrassing, a show-up.
Katie:	Embarrassing, but like I said, I had no choice ...
Interviewer:	I know a few people who have had to use them.
Katie:	Yeah, I've had to do it. I've even said to her go down and see if you can get another one because I'm just so, I'm in debt to my eyeballs, I've got loads of debt ...

Food bank vouchers in the city in which the research was conducted are normally limited to three per year, but these can be extended if a client is facing exceptional hardship. A voucher could be redeemed at any food bank outlet in the city. Katie had been given three vouchers during the period she was paying the Bedroom Tax. She described how the quality of food varied between different food banks, and stated that Ellen had travelled to another part of the city to redeem her voucher at a bank that distributed a better variety of food, including meat. However, another reason why Ellen travelled further afield may have been to avoid the embarrassment of using the food bank in the local area. Poverty is stigmatising for adults and children alike. Teresa, a single mother of three girls, described having to cut back on the lunch money she gave her daughter for school. Free school meals are available for children whose parents are in receipt of benefits, but research has revealed that many fail to take up this entitlement, in part because of the stigma attached to it (Dowler et al 2001; Caraher and Dowler: 2005). Teresa recounted having to restrict the amount of money she gave to her children and was finding it difficult to maintain payments for out-of-school activities:

> 'Yeah it's my oldest more than anything cus she gets a few quid, she doesn't like to get her school dinners, she gets a couple of quid. I was giving her a couple of quid you know, we've had to cut right down on that; she had three quid a day just for her lunch and whatever so she's definitely feeling it. Karate, well I did pay for karate last week, she's gone back to karate again, the eldest, I have to try and pay for the youngest when I can, I do try (sighs).'

Parents spoke about no longer being able to afford 'little treats' or pocket money, as Cath and Louise explained:

> 'That extra thirty pound, literally, even if it is once a fortnight, even if it was just a little treat like McDonalds, everything, no matter what which way we work out how to budget it, now they lose out cus we ain't getting no treats, there ain't a treat at all.' (Cath)

> 'My kids don't get pocket money, they don't get pocket money, they don't get taken anywhere. If they do get taken anywhere it's, do you know, what can we do cheap or what can we do free, and once, which is all good and well doing stuff free, but when you get to these places, they're places where they have to buy stuff, like an ice-cream. You can't have an ice-cream, I can't afford it. I mean we went to the park a couple of weeks ago and two pound an ice-cream, that's ten pound for five ice-creams, it's ridiculous, so you can't even enjoy yourself on a day like that because you're thinking "God, I've just spent ten quid on ice cream".' (Louise)

Eric had abandoned his home before he was evicted and had managed to secure smaller accommodation from another housing association in a different borough. In trying to minimise the consequences of relocation for his children he had kept them enrolled at the same school. Eric did not want to talk about how the move had impacted on his children. He said "it's not ideal but they seem all right". Eric was relieved that he had managed to secure a property for them to live in, as he had faced the prospect of homelessness. He talked about the stress this had placed on him and how this burden had been lifted now that he was no longer liable for the Bedroom Tax. Despite the fact that children are adept at hiding their own needs when family tension arises from poverty (Ridge 2011), those who relocate may also feel a sense of sadness and loss of their former home, friends and neighbourhood. Ellen described the experience of leaving her former home as "heart breaking". Upon relocating, Eric's children had to commute some distance to and from their school; at the time of interview Eric said that he was managing this. However, Eric is currently trying to relocate back to Tarley, as the initial relief of housing security has given way to a sense of dislocation from the supportive networks of family and friends.

Ridge (2011: 76) asserts that 'where parents are stressed children were also likely to be stressed'. As mentioned, stress and anxiety levels began to rise among participants who were in arrears and were receiving letters from the housing association about possible repossession. Betty had lived in her three-bedroom house for 17 years. She had moved into Tarley from another city after fleeing domestic violence. Betty had been allocated the house with her two sons and, while there, had her third son, who was now 14 years old. She spoke about moving in with nothing but the clothes on her back and how she and her sons had managed to build a new life for themselves. Betty suffered severe mental health difficulties and was getting some support from a mental health team after a recent breakdown in her condition had left her feeling suicidal. She talked about how her son did not want to move:

> 'He said, "Mum if we didn't have to pay this rent, we could stop here." I said – cus he don't really wanna move, I brought all me kids up here … "Why can't we just stop here?" I said "Well son, it's the money" …' (Betty)

Betty was hoping to downsize to smaller accommodation, as she was struggling to pay the Bedroom Tax. The stress was visible in her face and she spoke about how she was in a constant state of anxiety, saying that her son was now opening all her letters because she was finding the situation difficult to cope with. This anxiety is likely to have affected her son, who, at the age of 14, now had to shoulder the burden of relaying correspondence to his mentally ill mum to try to shield her from some of the responsibility. Similarly, Ruby said she had begun hiding correspondence received from the housing association because her teenage son had been reading it and getting himself "into a right state". A report by UNICEF asserts that 'children rarely manage to sidestep the stress and suffering of parents' and states that in the period 2008 to 2012 children in the UK experienced an 'unprecedented increase' in severe material deprivation, as measured by the ability of a family to pay their rent, heat their home and afford a reasonable diet (UNICEF 2014). This was before the implementation of the Bedroom Tax in 2013 and the subsequent hardship that has persisted for those affected. UNICEF estimates that since the start of the recession in 2008 the UK has lost six years of progress in tackling child poverty. Before the onset of the financial crisis, child poverty rates were decreasing in the UK a result of New Labour's redistributive policies. While analysis of austerity policies and their impact on children is ongoing, 'it is clear that children have been major losers in the aftermath of the recession' (Bradshaw et al 2017: 294).

Ten months after the introduction of the Bedroom Tax, Betty was able to downsize to a two-bedroom property within the neighbourhood. The house she vacated has no doubt been let to a family in need of accommodation. This is one of the principles of the Bedroom Tax: that it frees up accommodation for larger families experiencing overcrowding. In this sense, a family with children have gained. However, this has been to the disadvantage of children who, through no fault of their own, have been displaced from a home they did not want to leave, and after months of anxiety and adverse emotional effects. It remains open to question to what extent it is 'fair' if one child gains, but at the expense of another, especially when expanding the overall pool of affordable social housing was, and remains, an alternative.

There is evidence that the transmission of insecurity onto children is damaging, affecting them materially and emotionally, in turn having a negative impact on their ability to thrive at school (Bragg et al 2015). Children have not remained untouched by the Bedroom Tax: they are, along with their parents, facing adverse and potentially damaging material and personal impacts:

> Poverty penetrates deep into the heart of childhood, permeating every facet of children's lives from economic and material disadvantage through the structuring and limiting of social relationships and social participation to the most personal often hidden aspects of disadvantage associated with shame, sadness and the fear of social difference and marginalisation. (Ridge 2011: 73)

Children are not just suffering the material disadvantages of poverty; the impact of the Bedroom Tax is causing emotional distress as insecurity about housing is diffused throughout the household. The anxiety of parents who are finding it increasingly difficult to cope under the pressure of welfare restructuring is being transmitted onto children. Since 2010, child poverty rates have sky-rocketed, and are set to continue on this path – a consequence of the tax and welfare reforms implemented between 2010 and 2017. By the year 2022 this will result in 1.5 million extra children living in poverty (EHRC 2018). David Isaac, chair of the Equality and Human Rights Commission, said:

> It's disappointing to discover that the reforms we have examined negatively affect the most disadvantaged in our society. It's even more shocking that children – the future generation – will be the hardest hit and that so many will be condemned to start life in poverty. (Isaac 2018)

Add to this the bleak social mobility outlook for Britain's working-class children, and the future of a whole generation of young people looks set to worsen. As Lisa Mckenzie made clear in a debate for the Oxford Student Union, "the class system is static ... social mobility is a lie ... meritocracy does not happen ... there is no movement" (2017: 00.06.34). In 2014 the Social Mobility Commission's State of the Nation report warned that:

> 2020 could mark a watershed between an era in which for decades there have been rising living standards shared by all and a future era where rising living standards bypass the poorest in society. If that comes to pass the economic recovery will not have produced a social recovery. Social mobility, having flatlined in the latter part of the last century, would go into reverse in the first part of this century. The United Kingdom would become a permanently divided nation. (State of the Nation 2014: v)

Since this warning, nothing has changed, resulting in all four social mobility commissioners resigning their posts in protest at a lack of meaningful action in addressing the deplorable state of social mobility in Britain. Children are the hidden victims of austerity, not just spectators of their parents' anxiety; they too become burdened by financial hardship, the victims of a downward spiral of poverty and housing insecurity. The fracture lines between the haves and the have-nots are growing ever deeper and the divisions within society will have social consequences. One of the major drivers of social mobility is the housing market but, as insecurity in the social rented sector continues to be undermined by cuts to Housing Benefit and the PRS turns it back on those who rely on rent support, housing precarity is closer to becoming a defining feature of life for the low-paid and most economically marginalised. While this chapter has shed light on the adverse health consequences and the detrimental impact on children and young adults that housing precarity engenders, there is every reason to believe that this is going to be a continuing and growing consequence of the cutting back of rental support, particularly when the impacts of the Benefit Cap and the full roll-out of UC begin to take effect.

Conclusion

This chapter has addressed the question of how participants adapted to the Bedroom Tax policy from the date of its implementation in April 2013. Behaviourally, of the 31 participants who took part in this study, 27 did not initially seek to downsize from their properties. A number of participants expressed confusion about the policy and withheld payment of the Bedroom Tax because they did not understand why they were liable to pay. Others had not realised until they began receiving correspondence from their housing association that the policy had come into effect. However, the majority of participants responded financially by paying and attempted to keep up their payments. Despite their attempts to absorb the extra rental outgoings, many began to accrue rent arrears as they prioritised other household bills and the needs of their children over paying. The implementation of the policy resulted in the accumulation of hardship by adding a significant expenditure to household budgets that were already finite. Beyond impacting materially and financially, the policy impacted on the psychological health of participants as the accumulation of arrears and the ongoing pressure to pay resulted in heightened levels of worry and stress. The Bedroom Tax undermined housing stability, intensifying feelings of insecurity, as arrears represented a breach of their tenancy agreement. This insecurity was transmitted to children as parents failed in their attempts to maintain and present a facade of normalcy. As Ridge (2011) makes clear, children do not just stand as silent witnesses to the sufferings of their parents. At times they have to shoulder the burden as they live with the deterioration in a parent's psychological state. The findings in this chapter are part of a growing body of evidence that disputes the claim that the policy would have no impact on health and wellbeing. In the next chapter the focus shifts to explore the experiences of participants as they sought to downsize. This change in behaviour was a response to the impacts participants encountered, as detailed in this chapter. Having as its central theme the issues surrounding mobility within the social rented sector, the next chapter explores the structural constraints that further increased participants' vulnerability to housing insecurity and homelessness.

4

Social housing insecurity as policy and ideology

The Bedroom Tax policy did not specify that social housing tenants *had* to downsize. On the contrary, it gave them choices. They could look for employment to improve their finances, or they could absorb the extra cost, take in a lodger or move to smaller accommodation. In this regard, the subject had agency and was given the option of exercising it. Nevertheless, as has been shown in the previous chapter, downsizing was not something most participants chose to do. Participants were not passive in response, and their commitment to trying to remain in their homes could be read as a form of resistance to the policy. Some stopped paying altogether, while others adopted a 'we will not be moved' stance, echoed in the insistence by some that the only way they would leave their homes was 'in a coffin'. It was only in the context of deepening housing insecurity, as arrears accumulated, that action to downsize was taken. Nineteen of the participants had fallen into rent arrears. The situation had become so untenable for ten of the participants, and their housing situation so precarious, that they felt that they had no other option but to downsize. In the search for security and permanence, participants sought to find alternative accommodation. At the same time, the types of agency they could engage in were restricted by personal and structural constraints.

Drawing on the work of Wacquant and Foucault, this chapter adopts a more theoretical analytic framework to question how, and in what ways, the restructuring of the social security system abets the 'reengineering of the state' (Wacquant 2013: 8). The Bedroom Tax policy provides a lens through which to view how this process contributes to the spread of urban marginality through a deepening process of housing insecurity. How do you reconfigure the relationship between the subject and the state so that the populace comes to reimagine the role of the state from one which grants its citizens protective welfare as a matter of right (Wacquant 2012) to one which will 'systematically remove alternative means of support in order to enforce (low) wage dependency' (Peck 2001: 12)? In what follows, I analyse the relationship between structure and agency and how increased housing vulnerability impacts on participants, acting to responsibilise them and make them accountable for their own housing provision. Seen as a failure to manage, the internalisation of housing precarity socialises the subject to accept less from the welfare state and reinforces a reconfiguration of the purpose of social housing.

Resisting displacement: home and neighbourhood ties

Despite the difficulties some participants experienced in paying the Bedroom Tax, the majority attempted to 'stay and pay'. There are various reasons why, but mainly participants spoke about their homes as more than just bricks and mortar; they were family homes which they had invested in over many years. They were also fearful about what sort of property they would be moved to and worried that they would have no choice but to leave the neighbourhood. Participants had a keen sense that social housing was in short supply and worried about being moved to a 'rougher' part of the neighbourhood. The edge of Tarley, known as Tarley Wood, was once seen as the most desirable part of the neighbourhood. However, over the years, and as the drug economy gripped the area, Tarley Wood had declined and become infamous as a site in which crack dens proliferated. Further, participants who had lived in their homes for decades feared being moved onto other housing estates similar to Tarley. Considering that the city's 'priority' neighbourhoods are all areas with high levels of social housing, they felt safer in the one they knew.

The anger of some participants was palpable when they discussed having to move out of their home. Nadine, a 44-year-old mum, swapped houses with a woman across the road. She spoke sadly about leaving what she said had been a well-loved family home; their pet dog was buried in the garden. She had found it particularly upsetting when the woman from across the road brought her children over to look at the property and they had looked around, deciding which bedrooms they would have. People had invested in their homes over many years and the majority wanted to remain in them. However, this was about more than leaving a cherished home where a family had been raised and memories made. Participants were also uncertain about what type of property they would be moved to. Bob articulated this angrily:

> 'And they're people here that have had to move out their houses that have lived here for years, they've brought up their kids and everything [they have] had to downsize, but it ain't a matter of that. OK I've got a three-bedroom house, I don't want to be put in some poxy bedsit, flea-bitten

shithole, you know what I mean? This has been my home
and my kids' home and I ain't moving (voice rises) … I'll
burn it down first. I would, I wouldn't give a fuck … Like I
said, I won't leave this house unless I'm in a fucking wooden
box now, ain't giving this house up for nothing …' (Bob)

Participants could not afford owner-occupation and had no desire to
rent in the private sector because of the insecurity of tenure, higher
rents and the requirement for credit checks, references and deposits.
The security afforded by social housing had meant that they could
lay down roots, and this was why they had invested in their homes,
as Billy explained:

'How would I feel? I'd be literally gutted, literally, especially
building, it's like if – I know you're a young lady – but say
if you had been in your house 20 years, done it how you
wanted to, I'd be literally gutted I would. I think my wife
would be really seriously ill, personally, without a doubt, I
reckon she would be really ill.' (Billy)

Cath was not averse to moving but explained that the lack of social
housing limited the choice of where and what she would be able
to bid for. It was the case that tenants wanted to remain in Tarley,
showing a strong attachment to place. Knowing people and being
known was an important element that made living in Tarley preferable
to becoming a stranger on another housing estate, especially in
another neighbourhood which might have greater social problems
than the one they were in. Cath and her friend Julie discussed this
and alluded to the fact that many 'nicer' areas of the city had very
little social housing:

Cath: […] Yeah look at it, cus we've been here all our
                lives, I've grew up in this street since day one and
                that's why I've never moved out really, apart from
                Morgan road, when I lived up there for a year, and
                that was it.
Interviewer: So you wouldn't like to move out?
Cath: No, I'd like to, but I wouldn't get my choice, so,
                you know, they would give me [names another
                housing estate on the other side of the city], so I
                wouldn't be able to say Pilton [nice area] or …
Julie: They're hardly any council houses there anyway.

Don used his 'spare room' for his daughter, who stayed with him at weekends and school holidays. Don and Cath, like the majority of participants, had lived in Tarley their entire lives. Don said that the reason he had been allocated a two-bedroom flat in the first place was precisely because he had his child staying over. For Don, having to move to a bedsit or a one-bedroom flat could mean seeing less of his child:

Interviewer:	Did they give you any options, did they say you should downsize or …
Don:	They did say that, but how could I have my daughter at the weekends? She's always coming round and staying at the weekends. Sometimes she's here all week, sometimes here for five weeks on the trot during the school holidays.
Interviewer:	Did you say that to them?
Don:	Yeah, they didn't care. They don't care, basically. I just have to pay it. There's no way around it.

Participants with children felt that they should not have to downsize because all of their bedrooms were occupied. Cath, Louise, Teresa and Lisa had children occupying bedrooms but, because of the clause stating that children of the same gender can share until age 16, they were liable for the Bedroom Tax. Children under the age of 10 are also expected to share a room, regardless of gender. Cath had to pay as her two older daughters were under 16. Lisa had two sons aged 14 and 4. She expressed disbelief that a small child who went to bed early should be made to share a room with her older son, whom she described as a 'stroppy teenager'. Moving to a two-bedroom flat or house, which would involve putting the two boys together in a room, she felt, would be detrimental for them both and an absolute waste of time, given that two years down the line the age clause would be redundant when her son turned 16. Teresa had three daughters, but her eldest child lived with her grandmother across the road in a two-bedroom flat. Teresa and her daughter had a difficult relationship. However, she still saw her every day and they ate meals together most evenings, sharing the cost of food: "we work as one household", she stated. Moreover, Teresa's daughter's residence at her grandmother's flat meant that the grandmother was not liable to pay the Bedroom Tax, as Teresa explained:

Teresa:	I moved in with two and then as soon as I moved in I got pregnant with the third, so, and that was

> sound ... my eldest ... she moved over there with my mother, which stops my mother being liable for the tax.

Interviewer: How old is your mum?

Teresa: My mum's 55, even though she doesn't work, but like I said, cus my oldest sort of lives there it stops that, but my mum said before she went this morning, she said, 'I wouldn't even think about putting the girls back in the same room together' because the way they are all out at the minute my youngest ... it would be hell ... bad enough as it is and I don't have to share a room with her, she's a cow. I mean, I know teenagers are supposed to be trouble but it's ridiculous.

The majority of participants had family living close by. This was another reason why they wanted to remain in their homes. Older tenants often helped out by looking after their grandchildren and felt that if they did downsize they would have no room to accommodate them. Friendship, family and kin networks are an invaluable source of support which helps to alleviate the problems associated with poverty. For Emily, who had no relatives around her and who had numerous physical and mental health problems, even the local children who lived nearby were a source of support, as they would run errands to the shops for her. The importance of rootedness in home and the immediate locality is captured in Richard Hoggart's reflection on working-class life in the 1950s:

> The more we look at working-class life, the more we try to reach the core of working-class attitudes, the more surely does it appear that the core is a sense of the personal, the concrete, the local: it is embodied in the idea of, first, the family and, second, the neighbourhood. This remains, though much works against it, and partly because so much works against it. (Hoggart 1957/1992: 33)

Much continues to work against the working-class and their ability to remain 'fixed' in place (Paton 2013). As Hoggart recognised, family and neighbourhood are important. There is a failure underpinning the Bedroom Tax, which ignores the importance of home and neighbourhood and the psychological and material connections between them (Bragg et al 2015). It ignores too, the wider structures that keep people 'fixed' in such places: booms and busts in the economy, deindustrialisation, housing need and local housing allocation systems that facilitate the maintenance of close family proximity within neighbourhoods. Interviews with participants left little doubt that housing stability, family and neighbourhood were the only concrete things in their lives. Low-waged, flexible employment, particularly for lone parent-headed households, could not free them from their reliance on Housing Benefit or act as a catalyst for social mobility. Studies of the policy attest to the continued resonance of Hoggart's observation; the central reason for not wanting to downsize was that tenants were concerned that it would undermine family, friendship and neighbourhood ties (Bragg et al 2015; Clarke et al 2015; Gibb 2015).

At the same time, in a context of deepening housing insecurity, the sense of stability that social housing had provided was being undermined:

Nadine: I know you don't own it, or anything like that, but (sighs) the government have made us feel secure in our homes, they've made the, these social housing our homes. You know …

Interviewer: Yeah.

Nadine: It may look tatty to somebody else, but this is our home, you know, and, and that's it, and, like I say, you get your repairs done, and all that sort of thing, and, you know, it does make you secure … But, but they've took all that away now.

Despite the efforts of participants to remain in their homes it became increasingly difficult for them to do so. The reality was that staying in their homes led to food and fuel poverty, and the intermittent failure to prioritise paying the Bedroom Tax resulted in rising rent arrears that undermined the tenancy agreement. Correspondence and phone calls from the housing association warned participants that they were putting their tenancy in jeopardy, which could result in court action and a possession order being made on the property. This ongoing pressure galvanised some participants into initiating the process of downsizing. However, as is demonstrated in the following section, this process was not a straightforward one.

Mobility within the social rented sector

Media, the main housing provider in Tarley, had a policy whereby any tenant with rent arrears was not eligible to move. This also appeared to be the case with smaller housing associations. This left tenants who had accrued arrears in a catch-22 situation, as they could not afford to clear arrears but could not move either. At the very beginning of April 2013, just as the Bedroom Tax was being introduced, Mary was given help by the Law Centre to access a charitable fund which cleared her arrears and enabled her to move. After the implementation of the policy Mary's arrears increased and, if she had not been given any help, it was certain that she would have eventually been evicted, given that she was on JSA and was struggling to pay £24 a week in Bedroom Tax. Mary's previous rent arrears had accrued because she had spent time in prison, during which her Housing Benefit claim had not been renewed. Mary was subsequently able to move to a one-bedroom property around the corner. However, for others no help seemed to be available, or, if it was, they did not know how to access it.

Jessica, for example, was paying the Bedroom Tax sporadically and had started to panic about her arrears when she received letters notifying her that court action was being taken. At the time of interview she was in £520 arrears. She needed to move as quickly as possible to avoid losing her tenancy but did not know where to turn for help. She had been to the local Money Advice Centre and had been advised to phone the Law Centre, but had been unable to get through. I asked her if she had applied for DHP, but she was unaware of it – a response that was repeated by almost every participant interviewed. The Socialist Party had held a meeting to highlight their anti-Bedroom Tax campaign in the city and, at a local meeting held in Tarley, they said that they were available to help with filling in DHP forms. I informed them that my research suggested many tenants did not know about the fund and, in December 2013, the leader of the Socialist Party submitted a Freedom of Information letter to the council asking how much they had spent in DHP. The response revealed that only 35% of the DHP budget had been spent. However, it was not until January 2014 – 10 months after the Bedroom Tax had been introduced – that tenants received a letter informing them specifically about the fund and how they could apply. Jessica applied to the fund and they agreed to clear her arrears and pay the Bedroom Tax until March 2014. This would enable her to move, but in the meantime she still had to attend the county court hearing dealing with the possession order she had been served. Because her arrears were going to be cleared the possession order was suspended, but attending court proved an extremely stressful experience for Jessica. Upon leaving the court she said: "I need to get out of that house as soon as I can, I can't go through that again." Jessica then had to get help to access and navigate the online Homefinder website, but she had no idea how to use a computer or the internet and had no internet access, so she found this difficult. The ever-increasing move to web-based application systems within housing services and benefit claims – 'digital-by-default' – makes life much more difficult for those who are computer illiterate and have difficulty accessing the internet. Jessica subsequently bid on and managed to secure a one-bedroom flat. Her experience is captured in the following field diary extract.

FIELD DIARY
21 April 2014

I take Jessica to the Housing Benefit Office in town today, she texted me yesterday to tell me she had been offered a flat and that she needed to find out how to go about getting help with moving costs. It's easier to just go down there because it's really hard to get to speak to someone when you ring the office. We went to look at where the flat was first. It's in a low-rise block at the bottom of the hill. Jessica comments that it might be a bit too far from the shops. I mention there's a bus stop across the road but she's still not sure what to do and says she's feeling really down about it.

We went to the housing office and asked the receptionist about help with moving costs and explained that Jessica is downsizing due to the Bedroom Tax. The receptionist handed her a form and explained that Jessica should apply for a community grant; this had to be done online she said and pointed out the email address. Jessica looked even more despondent after hearing this and said 'Why can't I just speak to someone, I'm trying to do everything I can to move and no one's helping me'. I told her I would help her fill out the form that evening on my computer. I also asked the receptionist how many properties Jessica could refuse before she lost her priority status but she said she didn't know. Afterwards I took her round to a flat whose occupant was looking to swap properties with Jessica. Jessica said she would look at the flat, I showed her where it was but she didn't look impressed from the outside. We then went round the corner to her friend's house because they were going to see the flat together. Her friend Ruby had seen the flat and told Jessica she was sure she would like it but that she would need to get used to the smaller dimensions of the property. Jessica just sat there looking

really sad and teary eyed and said 'I've got used to my own house'.
Ruby noticed, but busied herself making tea.

Jessica accepted the flat she was offered. It was her first offer and she took it because she did not want to be moved out of Tarley and was aware that DHP payments would shortly be coming to an end. She was turned down for a community care grant from the DWP to help with removals but did receive a decorating grant from Media, which enabled her to buy some paint. Jessica's move was difficult for her, particularly having to phone utility companies to connect the gas and electricity supply. Often she would be placed on hold, which used up her mobile phone credit. Jessica's financial situation after moving was such that she had to get a food parcel from the local food bank. Nonetheless, at the time of writing she had begun the process of settling in to her new flat because, she said, "you just have to get on with it". Mary took longer settling into her new home. For the first few weeks she was tearful and sad. She was able to recruit family and friends who had cars to help move some of her bigger household items, while her other belongings were carried through the few streets to her new property. Mary was frustrated that the blinds and carpets that she had in her previous property did not fit the dimensions of the new one. When she could not get her TV set up properly on her first night in her new home she broke down in tears, saying, "I'll be fine if I just get the telly working". A few months after moving in Mary said she was happy, and called her new property her "forever home". At the age of 59 Mary hopes she will live out her days there without ever having to move again. It was the case that some of those who were able to secure accommodation within the neighbourhood eventually settled into their new home within a matter of months. Although the process of moving was stressful, they felt a sense of relief that they could still maintain social ties and friendship and kinship networks in a neighbourhood they had lived in for decades. Moreover, they were free from having to pay the Bedroom Tax, and therefore they felt more secure.

The constraints that participants came up against as they attempted to move, under conditions of financial hardship and rent arrears, were but one aspect of trying to downsize in a context where smaller properties were scarce. While participants were given greater priority on the housing list this did not alter the fact that there were very few suitable properties available within Tarley. Mick, aged 56, a participant with serious mental health problems, described living for months surrounded by his boxed-up belongings. Mick had been paying the

Bedroom Tax diligently, fully aware that any arrears could hamper his move. The fact that he lived out of boxes for months while searching for a smaller property is indicative of the constraints on how 'mobile' social housing tenants *can* be. When encouraging a more transient social housing population, policy needs to take into account the dearth of smaller properties, the costs to both tenants and housing associations of the actual process of moving and the powerlessness of tenants in relation to housing association rules and regulations. In this situation, participants felt increasingly insecure and what was previously a stable housing situation was turned into a state of flux.

A condition test also required tenants to have their homes in a condition that satisfied housing association officers before they could move. This ranged from decorating to repairs, including replacement of doors and light fittings. This placed a further financial strain on participants and was experienced as an unwanted intrusion that further demoralised them, as Betty explained when she had been told by a visiting housing officer to remove toilet stains with a toothbrush:

Betty: Oh, some of me wallpaper, though erm, a bit of wallpaper sticking up over the, the paper didn't paint, 'Oh that needs sticking down'. And she did say that. And then she went and – no, all the rooms are tidy, cus obviously I've got lads. Me toilet seat, just showed her the water marks and whatever, right.

Interviewer: Yeah.

Betty: 'Oh you'll have to get a, erm a toothbrush, and a bit of bleach, and clean that.' And I thought, 'You are having a laugh', you know what I mean?

Interviewer: How does that make you feel, when people come in your house and say that?

Betty: Well, I'll tell you how I felt, I was on a right downer I did, and I'm not, as I said, had to – getting all of this done and everything, and I seen that place, and I, I said 'I've spent all my money'.

Others avoided the inspectors by talking with housing officials on the phone or visiting the office in person. Some felt that the inspections were a form of surveillance and suggested that the real reason why housing officers were inspecting properties was in order to 'check up' on them. For some, like Cath, the inspection was a cause of embarrassment when the house had not been fully decorated:

'I've gotta go up there, but we need to sort these few bits out in the house, get the paint out upstairs and I'll show her everything. At the minute I don't really want her to come and have a look at that upstairs cus you can't afford to even upgrade on things.' (Cath)

The solicitor I spoke with felt that the condition test was, in his experience, another obstacle that stood in the way of tenants being able to downsize:

'I mean, one of the things that comes across, erm, it happens particularly with Media accommodation, is that what they will do is they will also say that you have to, you have to get past the condition test. So the condition of a property has to be acceptable, and what a lot of people are reporting to me is that actually, 'look it was in this condition when I moved in, it was problematic when I moved in, but they're now telling me that I have to do X, Y and Z'. And I, you know, I hope to God this was wrong, but I have a real suspicion that pressure is being put on those people, to try to improve their housing stock. Erm, in order to, in order simply to get them to be able to, well they're saying you need to be able to do this, this, this and this. And it is not their responsibility, the property was like that at the start, but of course none of these people, you know, I often find with middle-class people who come in to see me about something, they've already taken photographs of everything before they moved in, and they then give me a photograph of what it was like when they moved in. And they're holding it up, and use paper from that day [to show the date the photograph was taken]. You know, a lot of our vulnerable clients don't think that way. They don't think, you know, to protect themselves from that sort of thing. And so I've had a lot of people who were supposed to be moving or were going to move, erm, who've been told they can't, because of condition of the property isn't acceptable. And the works required are, I mean, I would struggle to finance the works required, so it's just impossible again, for some of them.' (Law Centre solicitor)

The 'condition test' became another obstacle to moving and prolonged the stress and anxiety about downsizing. It effectively meant that tenants were channelling money into improving the property while at the same time paying the Bedroom Tax, and this left them vulnerable to falling into rent arrears.

Untenable tenancies

Rent arrears, particularly for those such as Marlene and Eric, who were already paying off arrears steadily before the Bedroom Tax was introduced, was one of the main causes of eviction or abandoning a property. Eric was told he was unable to move until his arrears were cleared. He had identified a friend with whom he might have been able to exchange properties, which would have solved his under-occupancy and his friend's overcrowding, but his initiative was, he said, refused by Media Housing Association, as he explained:

> 'I would have swapped as well, helped em out, give somebody, it was Joe in fact, he wanted to swap with me, a three-bedroom for a four-bedroom, but they wouldn't let us do it because of rent arrears. Yet they want the house, they want me to move to a smaller property, but I can't because I've got rent arrears, so my rent was still adding up and I was refusing to pay it, I thought I ain't paying it.' (Eric)

In Eric's case, his rent arrears had risen so significantly because he had pre-existing arrears before the policy was enacted. Eric said that the previous arrears had resulted from making a new claim after his partner had left him, but he had been paying them back at a weekly rate that he could afford. However, the implementation of the Bedroom Tax had pushed him over the edge financially. As his arrears rose he began to feel helpless about the situation. Eric could not afford to clear his rent arrears, and the arrears meant that he could not move, so he just stopped paying. Even though this would mean eviction, he could see no way out of the situation other than abandoning the property.

I attended court twice with two different participants, Cath and Jessica. The following field diary extract provides a glimpse from a day in court with Cath and illustrates how other welfare reforms, such as the Benefit Cap, had caused another Tarley resident, Michelle, to fall into rent arrears. This, in turn, prevented her accessing housing that might have been freed up by the Bedroom Tax.

FIELD DIARY
14 November 2013

I go to the court to meet Cath and her former partner, Barry. They have had to attend county court today as they had received a possession order from Media because they have fallen behind with their Bedroom Tax payments. They both look tired and Barry tells me he hasn't been able to sleep all week, worrying about what's going to happen today. They meet with a solicitor from the law centre, he goes through the arrears with them and says, if they're willing to pay £40 a fortnight, which includes paying money off the arrears, he will ask Media to suspend the possession order. Media agree to this and they wait to be called into the courtroom. Cath is still confused about why they owe so much. We sit and wait in the waiting room and while we're there two more women from the same neighbourhood come in. Cath knows them. The older woman is called Marlene and she looks in a bit of a state. Visibly anxious and nervous, she tells Cath that she thinks she might lose her house today. I ask her what has been happening. She tells me she was already in arrears before the Bedroom Tax but had been paying them off a few pounds every week and now they say she owes hundreds. She seems confused as to why she owes so much money and has a big folder of paperwork, correspondence from Media, with her. She says that she wanted to downsize but, because of the arrears, was not allowed to move. She says she's 'trapped'. She said also that Media had told her she wasn't entitled to rent aid because she was in arrears. Cath said she is going to go to the Housing Benefit Office after court to apply for rent aid and DHP. She says Media didn't tell her that she could apply for this help. She says 'they're trying to clear the hood,' or in other words are using the Bedroom Tax as a way to get rid of undesirable tenants. I asked Marlene if she would speak to me about her experiences and she said she would. Barry is pacing about. He doesn't look well and he tells me his stomach ulcer is playing him up with the worry.

The other woman is called Michelle. I ask her why she's here because I know she has a large family so wouldn't have thought that she would have been affected by the Bedroom Tax. Michelle explains that she has been affected by the Benefit Cap; she's a single mum with seven kids living in a three-bedroom house. She now has to pay full rent on her Media property and has fallen behind with the rent and is in arrears. Because of this she can't move until they're paid off. She said 'I thought when the Bedroom Tax came in that I would get a four-bedroom place quicker and now because of the cap I can't move. I'm stuck in a rabbit hutch'.

The housing officer I interviewed claimed that no one had been evicted as a direct result of arrears accrued because of the Bedroom Tax. In his opinion the furore around it had died down and tenants appeared to have accepted and had learned to live with the new Housing Benefit cut. Moreover, he stated, a loophole in the original legislation had helped a lot of people to clear the arrears they had accrued. What is commonly referred to as the 'Bedroom Tax loophole' emerged around January 2014. It was a legislative oversight; a clause in the law had been overlooked which stated that anybody who had been living in the same property for 16 years and had been continuously claiming Housing Benefit should be exempt from the policy because of a clause relating to 'eligible rent'. The government stated that they would close the loophole by March/April 2014, but in the meantime those who were eligible could claim back the money they had paid and, in theory, clear their accrued arrears. The housing officer stated that this loophole had helped a lot of people to clear their arrears. However, in practice the threat of eviction was enough to frighten people into abandoning their properties before they were formally evicted.

Two of the participants in this study – Eric and Marlene – had been to court and had received notice to either clear arrears or be evicted and had simply abandoned their properties before bailiffs arrived. Eric managed to get a property in another borough, while Marlene moved in to her parents' house. In addition to these participants, Darren, as mentioned in Chapter 3, was formally evicted by bailiffs without having attended court, while, at the time of writing, Ruby was again in arrears, although she had successfully applied for DHP, which would cover her payments until August 2015. However, any future help from the fund is dependent on her actively seeking to downsize. Cath, who is in a four-bedroom property with four children, was, at the time of writing, facing the prospect of eviction if she did not settle her rent account. The government's evaluation of the policy found that by the autumn of 2014, 55% of tenants affected by the policy were in arrears (Clarke et al 2015). Many of those facing the threat of eviction simply abandon their homes like Eric did, and, as a housing solicitor highlighted, not all evictions ended up going through the courts:

'I suppose you would need to classify it in two ways. One is, I mean, not everything gets to the stage at which a judge turns around and says to that person, "You can no longer afford your rent, therefore I'm making a possession order to evict you from your home." A lot of people, erm, kind of realise that, they've had advice or they've had assistance and whatever it happens to be, they realise there's going to be no change to the Housing Benefit position for them. And they therefore either give up their tenancies, or whatever, so I would class that as still as, you know, those people I don't think would be classed as having been evicted, as such, but they certainly have lost their accommodation as a direct result of the Bedroom Tax. Erm, I think that now, that that's got to just beyond a year, since it, it all started, at the start there was a degree of sympathy from social landlords who were, they had policies, maybe, for helping people downsize or whatever. (Sighs) Personally speaking I think they were utterly shambolic. There was no cohesive policy across the board, erm, and they let the situation which, actually they were saying "well you can move, downsize to another property". But inevitably these people had either slight – some arrears from before or arrears since the Bedroom Tax. And they were using that as an impediment and saying "well you've got arrears". The situation there was we did successfully challenge some of those in the courts, which was to turn around and say "well that kind of policy inevitably leads to a situation in which you were always going to be evicted".' (Legal aid solicitor)

Meanwhile, on the other side of the city a 30-strong crowd of anti-Bedroom Tax campaigners surrounded the house of a man where bailiffs were standing outside to evict him from his home. The eviction was prevented by the protest and the housing association (Media) gave him a month to try to get a lodger. This shows that two years after the introduction of the policy some tenants were still struggling with the Bedroom Tax and continued to face the very real threat of eviction. The policy seems to assume a seamless reorganisation of people's lives and an amount of agency on their behalf that in practice is hampered by poverty, insufficient smaller properties and the apparently inflexible rules of housing associations, which combine to constrain mobility. How these people's lives are lived after eviction, being displaced or moving into a hostel is beyond the scope of this study, but the security of social housing which they once enjoyed has been lost or undermined.

Furthermore, this process works to spread advanced marginality deeper into their lives as they become cut off from, and set adrift of, the people and places in which many have spent their lives. They have lost not just their homes, but also the proximity of supportive social networks that were established over many years. They have lost a 'viable hinterland' (Wacquant 1996: 121) and now have to re-establish themselves in places where they did not want to be. Marlene, after being given 28 days' notice to pay off her arrears or have her house repossessed, seemed almost relieved that the months of stress, anxiety and uncertainty had come to an end, as this diary extract details:

FIELD DIARY
12 December 2013

Marlene was in court today. I went round to Cath's house and we went round to Marlene's house together to see what had happened and to make sure she was alright. Marlene was in a right state; she was drinking vodka, crying and ranting about what had happened at court. She said the solicitor acting on her behalf had given no defence and that the court had said she had 28 days to pay up or leave the property. She kept talking about how ashamed she was at having lost her home at her age (age 50). We managed to calm her down and I asked if she minded me turning on my Dictaphone so that I would remember what had happened. I hadn't yet had the chance to interview Marlene. She was fine with me doing that and proceeded to tell us what had happened. It was at times incoherent and she would jump from one subject to another. Her cat was sitting on the kitchen table and she said at one point 'what am I going to do with the cat?' Marlene got drunker and drunker; she looks like she hasn't slept properly for a long time. She also mentions that her disabled daughter, who lives in another city, won't be able to come and stay with her as she had hoped she would soon. I ask her what she's going to do and she says 'I'll have to go to my mum's'. I tell her about the anti-eviction network but she says she knows that bailiffs can come without any prior warning and she won't be sticking around to be thrown out by them and be publicly humiliated, she'll sell what she can and get out before the 28 days is up. 'It's all over now', she says, and I get the impression that she is relieved in a small way that a decision has been made because she has been having the stress and worry of eviction hanging over her for months. We stay at Marlene's for a few hours but I need to get home for the kids. I tell Cath that I'm a bit worried about leaving Marlene on her own as she is so upset. Cath says she can go with her and stay at hers for the night. I drop them both off in my car and head home.

While Marlene believed she had not been given enough help and support to maintain her tenancy, she also felt 'ashamed' that at the age of 50 she had lost her home and faced the prospect of homelessness. Marlene's arrears had risen to such an extent that she stood no chance of being able to pay them off. Even if she could have found the money, she still would have had to continue paying the Bedroom Tax unless she downsized to a smaller property. Marlene had become so ground down by her situation that it had exhausted her; it would have taken massive amounts of will-power on her part to go through the process of applying for DHP while searching online for smaller accommodation. She either had to do this herself or hand over responsibility to someone who was willing and able to take on the task of resolving her housing situation. Rather than put this responsibility onto someone else, she had fought to keep the home she did not want to move from. She bore the responsibility herself but ultimately failed to maintain the tenancy. Marlene moved in with her mum, dad and brother after she left her property; however, her relationship with her brother broke down and she rang me frantically one morning, crying and asking if I would accompany her to a homeless charity to see if they could help her find alternative accommodation.

FIELD DIARY

27 March 2014

I go and pick up Marlene from her mum's house. She is still very stressed. We go to the main homeless charity offices in town where I speak to a man at reception and explain Marlene's situation. The man is sympathetic but tells us that the charity is now only offering basic services. They have lost 20 members of staff due to cuts and another organisation based outside the city has taken over. This is the same service provider that is now in charge of offering mental health support to Betty, another of my participants. He advised us to go over to the housing office across the road and register Marlene as officially homeless. Marlene is still stressing out and I try to calm her down by saying that at least she is taking steps to find alternative accommodation. The housing office is busy. The woman at reception tells us that Marlene needs to use one of the phones on the wall to speak to someone and register as homeless. There are three phones; one is vacant and Marlene rings the designated number which is printed on a piece of paper on the wall. She explains her situation;

they take her phone number and tell her they will be in contact in about four or five days. While Marlene is on the phone I watch a physically disabled man who is anxious to use one of the phones; he is very agitated and eventually storms out, very upset, shouting 'I can't cope with this, I can't do this'.

Because Marlene was not living with any dependent children and was living with her mum she was viewed as having no immediate housing need. Marlene then 'sofa surfed' among friends. At our last contact, Marlene was residing in a homeless hostel in the city.

Walker and Chase (2014: 151) assert that in the UK 'recipients are repeatedly shamed by the presumption of their un-deservingness in the political rhetoric surrounding the rationale of welfare provision'. One tenant spoke about how he had taken 'stick' off some people for living alone in a three-bedroom property even though he was actively looking to downsize. Stigma and shame are becoming more pronounced as neoliberal discourses and welfare restructuring draw greater numbers of benefit-claimant groups into the category of undeserving poor. The Bedroom Tax depicts under-occupiers as undeserving, taking up more space than they need. While the depiction and rhetoric of welfare claimants as 'undeserving' has a long history in Britain, this discourse has become ever more pervasive and entrenched since the Great Recession of 2008–9.

Sheff (2000: 97) asserts that shame is 'the most social of the basic emotions', precisely because it is a relational emotion. Participants may know that their inability to manage is not simply a result of their personal failings, particularly when they are up against financial and structural barriers that impede their mobility. But it still induces shame because of how they think others will judge their situation. We need to view the emotion of shame within this context. Theorists have proposed that the 'action tendency' of shame is 'to hide, to avoid having one's personal failure observed by anyone' (Lazarus 1991: 244). Shame and stigma are intrinsically related to poverty and inequality – a finding supported by a growing body of literature that draws on social epidemiology and poverty studies (Wilkinson 1996; Wilkinson and Pickett 2009; Peacock et al 2013; Gubrium et al 2014; Walker 2014; Walker and Chase 2014). Those experiencing poverty are subjected to the deleterious material and symbolic consequences of both poverty and inequality. The tone of the debate surrounding Housing Benefit cuts invokes the issue of 'fairness'; it is not fair to those that cannot get on the property ladder, it is not fair to those who are in overcrowded accommodation. One participant, June, told me: "it's scary what they're doing and it's not fair". The majority of participants felt they were being unfairly targeted but were powerless to resist an ideological narrative that has an apparently common-sense lexicon.

> 'Now you realise what people do think of you, you know, as you grow up ... people do look down on you, even. I always found it cus if you work, it is understandable why people would look at you like that, but there ain't a job to go into, even if you go and study for years there ain't a job to go into, you know, like literally ...' (Cath)

Being unemployed and living in social housing represented occupying a valueless position in society. The only time Betty, during her interview, became animated and spoke with pride, was when she talked about her two older sons having jobs. Mark, similarly, spoke about his wish that his children would occupy a better position than him:

> 'Hopefully when they get older they won't be on the dole or on the council, they'll have a decent job, you know, make something of their lives, cus being on the council, being a council tenant and being on the dole is shit, it really is. Yeah, I don't agree with it, it's not nice, it's not a nice thing to have to do.' (Mark)

Some tenants invoked the notion of morality when voicing their opinion of the policy: "I didn't think it was morally right that I was living in a three-bedroom house on my own, when there's families crying out for houses" (Mary). Eric, similarly, used the language of 'fairness' when suggesting that a single person under-occupying by two rooms should downsize: "I agree that one person in a three-bedroom house, fair enough should give em a flat cus that suits them better." Participants drew on the rhetoric of fairness to frame the policy; in their narratives they allude within the dominant narrative to being 'lazy' or not morally entitled to take up more space than they require because they inhabit a supposedly 'welfare-dependent' community. They take on board the rhetoric and rationalise their position in relation to it.

To avoid shame, tenants had to displace themselves and abandon properties, to enact alternative strategies to ensure that they did not fall further into the margins, to avoid the feeling of public shame that eviction entails, to avoid that 'hidden injury of class', that feeling that '*you* aren't coping' (Sennett and Cobb 1973: 95). Shame, or the mere threat of shame, works to modify behaviour, in the process becoming a 'technique of the self' and the conduit through which neoliberal governmentality is enabled. Rather than being forcibly removed by bailiffs, those facing the real threat of eviction sold belongings and took what they could. They did the classic 'moonlight flit', moving on as secretly and as quietly as they could to avoid public eviction and escape from the rent arrears that had become such a burden in their lives, but in the process leaving a house that had been their home. They had to become responsible for making their own housing provision, as housing became a problem of 'self care', furthering the neoliberal logic of individual responsibility.

The participants in this study all had to deal with shaming encounters as they attempted to maintain their tenancies. They struggled to fill out DHP forms that required backdated bank statements and a list of living expenditures. They had to access home-finder websites when they were computer illiterate, make do without the basic essentials of toilet paper, ask for food vouchers and visit food banks. Murray (2009) maintains that 'stigma discourages dependence – it induces people to do everything they can to get out of the situation that put them in need of help'. Murray (2009) assumes that such experiences work to activate individual responsibility. What he and others like him fail to recognise is that, psychologically, 'shame is the most debilitating of the emotions, causing people to retreat socially, to lose faith in themselves and to find their sense of agency eroded' (Gubrium et al 2014: x).

There have not been any high-profile public evictions of vulnerable Bedroom Tax tenants in the national news. As this chapter highlights, this is arguably because many tenants either maintain their tenancies at whatever cost or abandon their properties once their level of arrears results in a repossession order. Governmentality emerges through 'techniques of the self' as individuals have to 'actively modulate themselves' (Lorey 2015: 70) and subjects that can adapt themselves to rapidly changing social situations are formed. In order to maintain a roof over his head when faced with eviction, Eric had circumnavigated the system and avoided eviction by relocating to another borough. He was not alone in taking such a step:

Eric:	Yeah, Jack's mum, she's gotta pay for two bedrooms, she's been in that house years, she's gotta pay for two extra bedrooms
Interviewer:	How old is she Eric?
Eric:	Fifty odd, about 56 I think.

Interviewer:	Is she still in the house they were in when they were kids?
Eric:	No, down Carter Walk, she's been there years anyway. She's meant to be moving out, she gets the keys on Monday, she's meant to be moving over here.
Interviewer:	Because of the Bedroom Tax?
Eric:	Yeah, she's moving because of that. Fresh start little flat, new house she's moving to.
Interviewer:	Is she in arrears?
Eric:	Yeah, she's in arrears, and cus you have to pay the council a certain amount of money to take rubbish away, her house is full of clutter so she'll be leaving loads so she'll be getting a big bill off em. She can't afford to pay it. She can't afford to pay anything else; she's taking what she wants and leaving the rest.
Interviewer:	A similar thing to what you've done then?
Eric:	Doing the same thing ...

Participants like Eric found themselves having to act strategically, finding ways to move but to remain in social housing despite their arrears. These participants had to become accountable for their own decisions; stay and pay, and learn to adjust, or improve their economic position by finding work, or else downsize. In much the same way that paupers entered the workhouse, the 'choice' was theirs to make. This is how neoliberal governmentality works; it is what enables the building of the neoliberal state. Individuals are subordinated while simultaneously being cast as agents of their own fate (Lorey 2015). In this way neoliberal societies become governed internally through 'normalising a general condition of precariousness' (Lorey 2010). The normalisation of housing precarity cements the normalisation of a reduced welfare state; if you cannot live within the means set by the state and/or behave in the appropriate way then what you can expect is further relegation to the margins: 'sofa surfing', homeless hostels, insecure private renting and displacement from your community.

As I watched Alfie literally shaking with anxiety as bailiffs, housing officials, protesters and local media gathered in front of the terraced home he had occupied for 40 years, I reflected on his bravery in trying to resist eviction. However, despite the victory of the protesters in preventing his eviction, and the efforts of anti-Bedroom Tax campaigners working on his behalf to keep him in situ, Alfie subsequently abandoned the property. One of the campaigners working with Alfie told me he had been 'embarrassed' by the furore that had surrounded his eviction. He moved to another borough, and is staying with a friend while he searches for accommodation in the PRS.

Reconfiguring ideas about the role of social housing

The value of secure social housing is often neglected in the government discourse that surrounds social housing policy. Rather than social housing being a contributing factor in 'welfare dependency' (Greenhalgh and Moss 2009), what it actually provides is housing security for the low-paid, those in precarious employment and some of the most vulnerable people in society. For many, however, the possibility of remaining was possible only because Housing Benefit provided the means to do so. Indeed, in this study, tenants such as Mary, Betty and Teresa had been allocated properties bigger than their needs because at that time these properties were 'hard to let' because of the run-down condition of some parts of the estate. They, however, were happy with their homes and had settled into them. Social housing gave them and their children security, they could put down roots and make and maintain friendship and kinship networks. The fact that, today, the sector now houses some of the most vulnerable sections of society – the sick, disabled and workless – means that any move to undermine housing security risks 'further disempowering households drawn overwhelmingly from the poorest and most disadvantaged sections of society, such that their prospects of ever establishing a stable home for themselves become increasingly remote' (Fitzpatrick and Pawson 2014: 611). Fitzpatrick and Pawson (2014) predicted that, even without the lawful authority of the 'fixed term' tenancies that housing associations can implement under the Localism Act 2011, the housing security of tenants would be undermined by the Bedroom Tax. This chapter has shown this to be the case. Security of tenure did give tenants the right to remain in their homes for as long as they wanted, but that was enabled only if the tenancy agreement was not breached by accumulating rent arrears. Reducing their Housing Benefit undermined their capacity to be protected by tenure rights. The government did not need to enact legislation that gave housing associations the right to impose fixed-term tenancies in order to encourage mobility within the sector; the Bedroom Tax did it for them, as it caused rent arrears which, if not paid, resulted in forfeiture of their tenure rights.

Despite the evidence of its harmful consequences (Rolnik 2013; Bragg et al 2015; Moffatt et al 2015) and apparent multiple policy failings (Gibb 2015), the Conservative government remains committed to the policy. It is portrayed as 'fair'. Why should social housing tenants live in properties with spare rooms? Why should the taxpayer fund them when there are other, needy families who are living in overcrowded conditions? This discourse lends the policy legitimacy, despite the profoundly problematic nature of the policy in practice. This may explain the reluctance of tenants to seek the help of anti-Bedroom Tax campaigners. They felt that the policy was unjust, but saw active resistance against it as futile:

> 'I think they just accept it, I think they just accept it cus I think they think the government ain't gonna change … policy or stuff, I think people just accept it. I mean, I've kind of accepted it, you know what I mean, so I suppose everybody thinks along the same lines as me.' (Annie)

Some tenants were aware that an anti-Bedroom Tax organisation existed in the city, but when I asked why she thought more people were not getting involved Cath responded:

> 'Because they're too frightened of losing their homes. I mean, there is a support group now for people who, erm, are being threatened with eviction through the Bedroom Tax. They're helping them out, but it shouldn't have been allowed in the first place.' (Cath)

Drawing on Foucault's concept of governmentality, Tyler (2015: 8) asserts that 'a major characteristic of neoliberal "democracies" is that they function through the generation of consent via fear and anxiety'; fear itself becomes a technology of neoliberal governance. How people manage under neoliberal governance and in the face of rising housing precarity is not through any great recourse to collective resistance, but by trying to maintain a level of 'resilience', self-management and acceptance under these conditions. Indeed, as O'Malley (2010: 500) states, 'resilience and adaptability have become central techniques of the self'.

Conclusion

In the UK, the project of austerity has centred on reforming the welfare state and tackling cultures of 'welfare dependency' and worklessness.

Under this new regime, social security assistance is conditional on a certain set of behavioural mandates used to coerce welfare claimants into the job market. The Bedroom Tax works on the same principle; by targeting only those under-occupiers who claim Housing Benefit, it aims to incentivise mobility and work. However, for many of those affected by the policy dealing with health-related issues, work was not a viable option. And, for many, mobility was not something they wanted, although it was something they did initiate as the threat of arrears and eviction forced their hand. In the UK context, housing policy and the reductions in Housing Benefit are key policy areas that assist in the modelling of the neoliberal state (Mayer 2010). Wacquant's argument that welfare state retrenchment advances urban marginality is useful here for understanding how a policy such as the Bedroom Tax has led to deepening marginality and housing insecurity. Those homes that have been vacated will provide a home for another household in need, while their former occupants search out alternative forms of shelter, sometimes far from their support networks.

The Bedroom Tax policy provides a lens through which to analyse what involvement actors have within the process of reconfiguring welfare states and the role they play in co-determining each other's emergence (Lemke 2001). The Bedroom Tax policy does not directly remove people from their homes. Tenants are given choices, and Housing Benefit is still available, but only at the price of behaviour modification. Tenants have to accept living on a reduced income or modify their behaviour through downsizing or finding work. Foucauldian concepts are useful theoretical tools for analysing how the behaviours of participants are shaped by deepening housing insecurity. Participants were not passive actors; they displayed expressions of resistance by withholding payment and refusing to move from their homes. However, these acts of resistance ultimately plunged them into deeper insecurity as they put their tenancies at risk. Once arrears accumulated, they had little choice but to act. Resistance intensified insecurity and individualised risk; they had to downsize, but their ability to do so was hampered by the structural constraints operating within the social rented sector.

Trying to move and navigate through the changing bureaucratic structures of the welfare state, the lack of face-to-face advice, itself a consequence of austerity cuts, and the policy of 'digital by default' intensified the sense of powerlessness. Feelings of failure and shame were the 'hidden injuries of class' that prevented people from trying to fight against eviction (Sennett and Cobb 1973). Participants had to displace themselves, take what properties were available, abandon properties and seek shelter in the homes of others. They ultimately had to take personal responsibility for the situations they found themselves in and make provision for their own housing needs. Gibb (2015: 148) asserts that the policy is a failure because of 'fundamental design problems' and its 'unanticipated consequences'. However, ideologically, one would argue, it has been a huge success. Increased housing insecurity became internalised, management of housing was shifted from the state onto individuals who quickly learned to accept what the state would provide, or else face the consequences. It is governance through insecurity (Lorey 2015); it personalises insecurity and people act on the basis of it. The whole process works to reconfigure ideas about social housing and conveys a simple message that 'you do not own these homes' and 'your benefit-dependent status gives you no right to occupy them'. In the following chapters I explore the way in which the policy positioned under-occupiers as not worthy of taking up more space than they needed because of their reliance on Housing Benefit and how the culture of blame which it encouraged impacted on localised relationships at the neighbourhood level.

5

Divisive social policy: the competition for physical and symbolic resources

The Coalition government's impact assessment of the Bedroom Tax policy, published in 2012, stated that there would be no social impacts resulting from its implementation. At best, this assessment was woefully ignorant of the meaning of stable housing in people's lives. Those affected by this policy were sick people, care-givers, those in low-paid work, parents and children. Materially, the policy left them in deeper poverty, or pushed them into rent arrears and the threat of eviction. Mary, who had been asking her housing association to help her downsize for years, was thrown into turmoil when the policy hit. Symbolically, this policy represented a decisive shift for those in social housing and it created despair, anger and rage. A common sentiment among participants was that the government had targeted a policy at them *because* they lived in social housing. They felt that they were a class looked down upon by wider society, the media and politicians.

This chapter illuminates how the discourses and rhetoric that surround 'welfare dependency' and social housing are experienced by those who are subjected to them by exploring how the Bedroom Tax is rationalised. It looks at how participants evaluate austerity politics in terms of their own economic position. It then turns to focus on their status and social positioning and on how the policy raises questions of worth and value. Participants' opinions about the policy and the effects of its implementation reveal that 'the social basis of respect' and access to 'valued ways of living are unequally distributed' (Sayer 2005: 954–5). What we see here are struggles not just over material resources such as housing but also over less tangible psychosocial and symbolic resources that give people a sense of worth and value (Sayer 2005; Skey 2014). When life outside of paid work is denigrated, when people who do work are judged not to be working hard enough and deemed less worthy than others, how do they stake claims to resources, dignity and respect? By drawing on Skey's (2014: 327) notion of 'hierarchies of belonging', I analyse how social positions allow for judgements and distinctions to be made about various 'others', and the ways through which denigration is deflected, and worth and value are recovered and asserted, through judgement, distinction and claims-making.

'People like us' and 'mingers like them'

Wacquant's (2007: 67) concept of advanced marginality includes processes of 'territorial stigmatization'. He outlines how stigma is spatialised, so that certain places are spoken of and become known 'as urban hellholes in which violence, vice and dereliction are the order of things'. While these negative representations serve to make such places the target for public policies, Wacquant argues that they also trickle down to the residents who internalise these negative portrayals. These discourses of 'vilification', in the UK context, can be observed most clearly in the rhetoric that surrounds Britain's social housing estates (Hancock and Mooney 2012; Tyler 2015), depicted as 'ghettos for our poorest people' (Duncan Smith 2009, cited in Slater 2014: 962). This wider narrative about social housing and those who reside in it was not lost on the participants in this study and there was a strong sense of stigmatisation, fuelled by the proliferation of 'poverty porn' and TV programmes such as *Benefit Street* and *Life on the Dole*. These portrayals of those on benefits were seen to homogenise tenants, depicting them all as workless. The rhetoric of hardworking families and hardworking people used by New Labour and subsequent administrations was summed up in the Conservative Party conference phrase 'for hardworking people'. Its implied opposite is 'workless', with social housing implicated as a causal factor to that workless state. Mary articulated the way she thought wider society viewed social housing tenants as engaging in a distinct life-style involving criminality and drug and alcohol addiction:

> 'They think all the people in social housing are on the dole, all the same, when we're not! We're not all out to drink our money, smoke our money, or take drugs and all the rest of it, all we wanna do is just get by, just to live out our lives ... just ... as you should do ... just get by. We don't have holidays abroad or ... I haven't got a flat-screen telly as you can see, I've got nothing, I don't need fancy things, I mean this is second hand (settee). Everything's second hand in my house, as long as it works, that's all I want. I don't need big fancy tellies, and stuff like that ... wooden floors and ... I couldn't have a wooden floor in this bloody place.' (Mary)

Others felt that they were looked down upon by politicians and the media, and spoke about their class position as being beneath the working class or, as Don put it, "the lowest of the low":

'I feel like they think that, like we're the lowest in society, so no, I … Like, it's as if, I can't think of the words, erm, beneath them.' (Tracey)

'Probably as scum I suppose … probably as we're lower class than them. I don't think we are, there are good people in these council places and stuff.' (Fiona)

'I think they just think we're like freeloading scumbags.' (Mark)

Tyler (2008: 32) argues that 'within the representational regimes which dominate within contemporary Britain social class is only visible in highly stereotyped and often antagonistic forms'. The words 'scum' and 'lowest of the low' vocalise a class positioning that is below that of the working class; a position that has no value and is looked upon with disgust. Katie's daughter and Louise outlined the stereotypes that proliferated within the media, and which they felt negatively portrayed them:

'As tramps! That *Benefit Street*, they think we are all like that. We ain't actually like that. It's disgusting. They think all people that live on estates like this are mingers like them. That's exactly what it is, ain't it? They think we are, like we're all druggies and smack heads and go out robbing houses and stuff like that.' (Katie's daughter)

'We all spit bars, we all know how to roll a spliff at the age of six, we got a mattress in the garden, although to be honest I do actually have a mattress in me garden (laughing). And there's all kids of different colours all hanging around the front door all calling ya "mum" – also that's my house (laughing), you gotta have a token black kid. I've got a token white one (laughing), oh God, white is the new poor (laughing). Funny, it used to be black was poor and now it doesn't matter whether you're white, purple, green or orange, we're all poor. Yeah, I just think the media's just … to the media we're all Jeremy Kyle-watching, uneducated, badly spoken, spliff-rolling, coke-snorting slags with 20 kids of all 20 shades with a mattress in the garden (laughing).' (Louise)

Louise's comment – 'white is the new poor' – suggests that white people are now occupying a lower position than they once enjoyed. It is a counter-narrative to that which positions black and minority ethnic groups as the most disadvantaged, and a resource drawn upon by those 'experiencing discursive exclusion and perceived injustice' (Hewitt 2005: 69). Hewitt (2005: 69), in particular, discerns such counter-narratives in some 'white working-class communities that perceive themselves to be economically under threat and/or without adequate mainstream representation'. For Louise, white people were now experiencing a devalued position and status that she, as a mixed-race woman, had experience of. She suggests this position was once experienced only if you were a person of colour. It is through a supposed 'welfare dependency' that welfare recipients lose aspects of their white privilege. Webster (2008: 307) asserts that 'class contempt towards economically and socially marginalised "white" groups reveals features of discourses and representations previously reserved for visible minorities'. Louise understands this, articulating that a certain form of 'whiteness' is being reconstructed as a new form of racialisation (Haylett 2001). Louise recognises the media's role in propagating such stereotypes and draws on historically gendered assumptions about working-class women. She describes the figure of the 'chav mum', a characterisation, Tyler (2008: 1) argues, which is 'produced through disgust reactions as an intensely affective figure that embodies historically familiar and contemporary anxieties about female sexuality, reproduction, fertility and racial mixing'. Indeed, the state's concern about working-class women's fecundity remains evident in its new restrictions on child tax credits paid to low-income women, which, as part of welfare reform, are now payable for the first two children only.

Participants did not just feel 'looked down' on by wider society, but pointed out how other people they knew held similar views about the unemployed, as Cath and her friend Julie discuss:

Interviewer:	Cath how do you think that the newspapers, politicians, and those in wider society, how do you think they view people who live in council houses?
Julie:	Scumbags!
Cath:	Yeah, down and outs like, bottom of the ladder. Do you know what, even people I've seen grow

up all their lives on benefits, now they put little status[1] on [Facebook] like 'people should get a job, stop taking our money blah, blah, blah', so if they look at us like that, well ... do you know, like the upper, upper class look down ...

Julie: They think we're spongers.

Cath spoke in a sad tone when she talked about how others who had occupied a similar position to hers spoke about people who claimed benefits. Being a worker is a valued position insofar as it is a position allowing one to make judgements over those who are not working. Cath did not just feel stigmatised by wider society, she also felt it from others with whom she had grown up but who could distinguish themselves from others because of their employed status. Cath recognised that this was a form of 'lateral denigration', drawing on the discourse of 'strivers' and 'skivers'. This highlights the 'intra-racial as well as inter-racial distinctions and exclusions' through which individuals distinguish who is deserving or undeserving of resources (Rhodes 2011: 107). To be unemployed is to be a 'taker'; someone who is not contributing becomes by extension part of a white working-class 'out group'. The status of being in paid work is a position from which moral boundaries can be drawn (Sayer 2005) and where people can assert their moral worth and value in relation to others. Participants may have felt 'looked down on', stigmatised and disparaged as 'undeserving', but some were also implicit in disparaging others within the neighbourhood, using the same discourse.

In the following extract Louise likens other families within the neighbourhood to the people who appear on TV shows such as *Jeremy Kyle* who are posited as unambitious, doing little with their lives except 'hang around'. She posits herself and her own ambitions in opposition to these families, drawing on notions of 'roughness' and 'respectability'.

'Because a lot of low-income families who like to ... it's terrible really cus I'm stereotyping them but they like to be a stereotype, they like to be a low-income stereotypical Jeremy Kyle family, if you can call it a family, and that's how they like to live, and I don't wanna live round people like that and raise my children around people like that. I want to be able to raise my children around people who are ambitious and adventurous and want to do stuff with their lives and not hanging round the precinct with pink hair and a cap ... no, couldn't do it.' (Louise)

Louise is employed, although because she is in low-waged work she is still eligible to claim a percentage of Housing Benefit to help with her housing costs. But it is through her employed status that she can make a claim to respectability, in opposition to those she sees as 'living on benefits', those who appear to have no aspiration. As Webster (2008: 302) observes, employment status has 'continued salience ... as a marker of class and respectability'. Skeggs (2009: 46) asserts that claims to respectability 'become key weapons in an armoury of defence' against being 'looked down on'. Employment, for Louise, is a primary resource she can draw on to distance herself from those who are wholly reliant on benefits; she may claim some benefits, but is not completely dependent on them financially. As such, she occupies a higher level on the ladder – one step above the disreputable workless. This is an effort on Louise's part to distance herself from the stigma and shame associated with so-called notions of 'welfare dependency'. As Shildrick and MacDonald (2013: 299) assert, 'those at the bottom *had* to imagine there were others below them', in order to avoid the 'symbolic degradation' that is associated with occupying a wholly benefit-dependent position (Wacquant 2009: 108).

Distinctions about behaviour were drawn upon by the local housing officer, who suggested that the 'white' working-class residents on the estate engaged in 'council estate behaviour' (Hanley 2012: 10). This revolved around acting in anti-social ways, being unemployed and failing to treat their neighbours and their properties with respect. Such distinctions draw on cultural representations rather than on the structural issues of unemployment and poverty:

> 'There's generations of families living here and the conversations going on within those families are 'why can't I get a Media house,' and it's becoming very multicultural around here. Do you know what, a lot of the African families, Polish families, all make good tenants, they're a lot more respectful to their neighbours, erm, they treat their properties better, erm, you know there's a good work ethic, erm, a lot of problems that we have are from your white British families.' (Media housing officer)

As stated in Chapter 4, housing officials visited tenants' properties to check the 'condition' of their homes; this placed them in a position where they could make visible judgements about tenants' lives. In the housing officer's account, these 'abject whites' are the 'problem' tenants; they are a problem community, who behave disreputably and lack the requisite 'work ethic' (Haylett 2001).

Most of the participants felt that the government had legitimated the Bedroom Tax policy through the rhetoric of 'welfare dependency' and that these representations were given added credence by poverty porn TV programmes and a wider discourse that contained classed assumptions of those who claim benefits and live in social housing. Such assumptions have become pervasive and entrenched signifiers of social class and an underlying pathology. Participants felt the 'symbolic violence' of this, but were also aware that it resulted in a symbolic divide between the employed and the unemployed or the 'striver' and the 'shirker'. This was something that was felt in everyday communication or in online forums. These are not benign messages or discourses, they are damaging to social relations; not only do they make people feel like valueless members of society but they are also messages that reverberate within the working class, becoming some sort of accepted wisdom and common sense. These discourses divide people from each other, undermining solidarity and the potential for collective resistance to social policies that are destructive to people's lives and communities.

The devaluation that participants felt was compounded by the feeling that mainstream political parties did not represent them or stand up for their interests. There was a widespread feeling of voicelessness, that politicians were completely divorced from their lives. While this made people angry, what shocked them was that the government would enact a policy that threatened so much: the very foundations on which they had built their lives, their homes and family and friendship networks, not to mention the situation it might put their children in. The 'housing question' that fired the indignation of philanthropists in decades before the state intervened in the housing market has once again reared its head, in the current housing crisis in the UK. But, arguably, what is lacking in these times is the rise of a labour movement that the working classes feel will fight for their interests and concerns – of which a major concern is the scale and pace of immigration and the perceived pressure that this places on housing, as the next section demonstrates.

'There's too many immigrants in this country'

Interviewer: Why do you think politicians brought it in, Jess?
Jess: Do you really want me to say?

Interviewer: Yeah, I want your honest opinion.

Jess: I think it's the foreigners they're bringing over, I really do. Like if they do chuck me out of here I can't see people that have been brought up here moving in with a family, I really can't. That's my opinion.

This interview extract highlights two themes that emerged strongly from the research data. Firstly, the hesitation of participants to articulate their honest opinion about why they thought the Bedroom Tax had been introduced. And secondly, the way participants linked the policy with immigration. They were reluctant to talk about 'foreigners' or 'immigrants', seemingly because they were unsure about voicing their true opinions. When talking about these issues, participants would often begin or interject that they were not being racist, rather, they felt that what they were saying was not an issue of ethnicity but that there was a dual problem of too many immigrants and not enough housing. They were, as a result, being forced out of their homes to make room for new communities. The hesitancy of tenants to express their opinions about immigration is underpinned by a perception that in doing so they would be viewed as racist, or even criminalised for holding such views as Emily, aged 52, explained:

'As far as I'm concerned they want me out of here so they can put them foreigners in here, and I know I shouldn't feel like but I am, I am. But if I said anything out there I'd get done for it.' (Emily)

Participants' attitudes towards minority communities were intrinsically related to housing. The neighbourhood in which they lived was, and is becoming, more diverse. The city, and the West Midlands conurbation more widely, is the second most diverse region outside of London. Participants felt that if the housing crisis was so bad that the government needed to free up spare rooms in their homes, in what for them was a process of forced eviction, then how could they house people coming into the country? Battiston et al (2014: 3) suggest that social housing 'is an area where immigrants and natives might be in more direct and visible conflict over access to resources'. Social housing does not work like other resources such as health and education, where funding mechanisms (despite their inadequacy) aim to ensure that increases in population are followed by increases in resources (Battiston et al 2014). In response to the accession of

12 new states to the EU, all previous regulations governing eligibility for an allocation of housing that were contained in the Housing Act 1996 were consolidated in the Allocation of Housing and Homeless (Eligibility) (England) Regulations, implemented in 2006 (Robinson 2008). These Regulations gave the following groups eligibility for an allocation of social housing: nationals of the European Economic Area (EEA), if they are working legally in the UK; asylum seekers given leave to remain in the UK; and other non-EEA state nationals who have satisfied the 'habitual residence test' (Robinson 2008). Research conducted by Rutter and Latorre (2009) demonstrated that there was no evidence to suggest that foreign migrants are favoured over British-born citizens. However, Battiston et al make the following observation:

> There is certainly no evidence of discrimination in favour of immigrant households as is believed by a sizeable fraction of the white British population. However, we show that there have been some important changes – the immigrant penalty has fallen over time. So, the combination of a rising immigrant population and a change in the allocation rules that benefit immigrants has combined with a declining social housing stock to reduce the probability of native households having access to social housing. (Battiston et al 2014: 1)

So, while greater numbers of those previously denied access to the sector began to occupy it, at the same time the stock of social housing was not increased. Battiston et al (2014: 2–3) suggest that this process 'means that one more immigrant household in social housing is quite likely to be one less native household. And this will be visible in a way that the receipt of welfare benefits is not.' While many of the participants in this study had parents who were migrants, the feeling of being 'pushed out' or 'forced out' was pervasive and they spoke with real anger and fear; it appeared to them that they were being forcibly removed from their homes to accommodate an ever-growing immigrant population. Research had already demonstrated that housing is one arena through which anger about resource competition is implicated (Garner 2009).

These feelings do not just inform how people feel at the micro level; they have real repercussions politically insofar as participants feel that the problem is one of immigration, leading them to vote for, and support, the policies of anti-immigrant political parties such as the British National Party (BNP) and UKIP. By supporting far-right populist parties, a small number of participants felt they could express electorally what they felt they could not say publicly. As Garner et al (2009: 9) observe, 'the implications of this for the political capital that can be accrued by the far-right are very grave'. To feel 'forced', 'pushed' or 'bullied' suggests that tenants felt a lack of agency and choice; they felt intimidated and coerced by a higher power. This higher power is seen as the government, but the reasoning behind the government's actions is perceived to originate in a need to house the perceived influx of migrants. This situation is then rationalised in such a way that it becomes a cause and effect relationship, or, put simply, the need to house migrants results in British-born tenants being forced to move in order to house them. Ruby articulated this line of argument:

> 'I don't know (laughs). Well, unless it's for all these ones that are coming into the country and they need to house them, cus they've got like hundreds and thousands of kids, basically, and that's not me being racist but it's like they're pushing us out, that were born here, to house them.' (Ruby)

Ruby articulates a sense of entitlement that being born in the UK should give her priority over newcomers. She states that it is not about being racist but that those who were born in Britain should have a stronger claim to entitlement. In existing research looking at white working-class communities, respondents often drew upon notions of entitlement insofar as anger towards new migrants was caused by the perception that they had not paid into the system and, as such, they were less entitled, particularly to housing (Dench et al 2006; Webster 2008; Garner 2011). However, because many participants were economically inactive, their entitlement drew more on 'indigenous' notions. Through being born in Britain, and their longevity in their homes and neighbourhood, they felt a sense of entitlement over others. This corresponds to the findings of Rhodes (2011), whose research with BNP supporters highlighted how economically inactive participants draw more heavily on claims to nationhood and locality when asserting their entitlement to resources.

Skey (2014: 327) argues that 'there is a strong link between belonging and entitlement, so that "I belong more than you" also means "I deserve more than you"'. The conceptual framework through which participants articulate entitlement is through belonging to the British nation and to their neighbourhood; they belong because they were born here and, for the majority, have lived out their lives in Tarley. The importance of this framework is that it provides 'an important sense of agency, in an era where growing numbers feel increasingly disenfranchised' (Skey 2014: 327). Welfare reform is not just being felt economically; it is also undermining participants' sense of space and place. As Mary suggests, their whole way of life is under threat as they face displacement from their homes and neighbourhood. The often complex language of austerity and budget deficits appears as nothing more than words used by politicians. For participants, what austerity means is struggling to keep their homes and remain in their neighbourhood and, while this takes place, new communities moving in appear to take the homes that they, because they claim Housing Benefit, are no longer entitled to inhabit. The Bedroom Tax policy positions tenants as less entitled to their homes because of their status as Housing Benefit claimants; they, however, position new communities as less entitled within a 'hierarchy of belonging' (Skey 2014). That entitlement to belonging is based on national identity and being British 'born and bred'; participants drew on that to stake a claim to social housing because it was one of the very few resources they had. In that way they also recovered some sense of value and recognition of being 'part of a group that lies at the heart of national life and culture' (Skey 2014: 326).

Three of the participants in this study used racist language; one stated openly that he was racist, suggesting 'we should send them all back'. These opinions were based on hate and ignorance, but overall the views expressed were nuanced and were made in direct relation to housing. Very few believed the Bedroom Tax policy was introduced to make better use of housing stock. The conversation often returned to the issue of immigration, with participants positioning themselves as the ones who were forced out of their homes because the government had failed to put in place enough housing for people. The context here is one in which tenants feel unsettled. They are negotiating a welfare system that can no longer guarantee them their homes and they are fearful of the future. Their response is one of hurt, loss and anger, which is directed at the 'others' in their midst – immigrants. As Holmes and Manning argue (2013: 494), 'in trying to make sense of the struggles to make ends meet some people turn to the racist discourses blaming immigration because few other resources are available'.

Louise, who described herself as mixed race, spoke at length during her interview about her own experience of being subject to racism. She articulates the same feelings about immigration as white participants. This appears to confirm the argument that 'we need to move away from popular analyses that identify ethnic or racial or national differences as the primary cause of conflict to examine the socio-economic and political context in which such conflicts emerge' (Skey 2012). Indeed, while the majority of participants in this study were white British, the effects of the housing crisis and cuts to Housing Benefit impinge on *everyone* on a low income relying on rent support. While Louise was more nuanced in her opinions, she still saw immigration as a problem:

'It makes me feel angry, it makes me worried for other people as well, because so many people are having to move from homes they've lived in all their lives. I mean the house that I live in, erm, before I'd moved into it was my grandparents' house. I moved into it to look after my grandfather and it's only ever been in our family, it's never been in anyone else's family. It's gone from being when Mabel moved into it, she moved into it fresh, she had her kids in it, raised her kids in it, then my granddad moved in and they raised Margaret, then we moved in. I've raised my kids there and I'm constantly thinking I need to move but move where? I feel like I'm being pushed to move out my house, and because I have no other ... I know other people who have been ... my sister-in-law, she's had to move, she can't afford the Bedroom Tax, into a two-bedroom flat. She's gone from being in a house she's been in from when it was built, erm, raised my nephew, he's now 14, 15, and has had to move into a flat ... I don't really pity myself because I suppose if I really wanted to I could change it, but it's the whole being bullied by the government ... having to move out of my house just so ... for what reason? What reason? What is my extra bedroom doing to you? Nothing, and it isn't even an extra bedroom, there's a bed and a body in it, it's just ridiculous. I just don't get it, I don't understand why it's happening at all, erm. I'm the last person to be racist in this world but I do think that we need to think about shutting our borders because all that's happening is ... this has happened because immigrants are coming into this country, having council houses, renting them out to different people, making money ... renting these homes out and this is why we now have a Bedroom Tax. Because we're being ... just being penalised for what other people are doing. Make them work for it or, it's hard because then if you've got a woman whose came from the Congo, who's, do you know, been raped, battered, abused or whatever, it's not about sending her home either. You've just got to find a steady medium, just filter out those that are here for bad gain and bad means, to the people that really do need it. But ... but you do, you just feel like you're being bullied to move so that maybe an immigrant can have your house with their 20,000 children. I've got enough children to have the house, I don't see why I should be bullied out of it but it's exactly what it feels like, and I feel a lot of people think that way, that they're being bullied out of their homes because they can't afford it, because we're all on benefits if we're working or not, cus people get benefits and if you can't afford it you can't afford it.' (Louise)

Louise alludes to immigrants "and their 20,000 children", and other participants also made the same over-inflated statements. Social housing is based on need, which is heavily influenced by family size. There was a perception that immigrants had larger families that acted as a gateway to securing social housing. The same prejudicial representation in political rhetoric and popular culture, that working-class women are 'excessively fecund' (Skeggs 2004: 11), was also being directed at migrant women. The extract from Louise also raises such issues as entitlement to a home that has been lived in for years and passed down through the family, which was enabled under the rules governing social housing allocation. Until the 1980s social housing allocation prioritised those with family or local connections (Garner 2009). As such, 'distinct patterns of settlement would be reproduced with extended families in proximity' (Garner 2009: 46). Close familial proximity also allowed for the informal welfare system to operate through local networks of care. Louise moved in with her granddad from a property around the corner to take care of him, as he suffered from dementia. While access to the social housing waiting list still works in favour of those who can show a local connection to the city, the shrinkage of social housing has made this much harder. The distinct local housing conditions within Tarley during the 1990s had enabled families to live within the same locality because the neighbourhood had been one of the most economically disadvantaged districts in the city. It had a reputation as 'rough', and the run-down state of some of the housing, particularly the early built 'no fines' housing, made it appear an undesirable place to live. This resulted in a situation whereby being allocated social housing accommodation within Tarley was generally unproblematic. Tenants had lived on the estate when it was an undesirable place to live, although subsequent regeneration and the more recent re-rendering of the 'no fines' housing had vastly improved the run-down look of the estate. The low-rise blocks of flats had been fitted with new balconies and the area around had been landscaped. The estate had never looked so good, while at the same time residents felt they were becoming less entitled to inhabit these homes. Betty, recalling the condition of the housing in her street when she moved there in 1997, stated, "they all looked derelict when I moved in, most of the houses where empty when I moved in here".

Within the local institutions of the community, anti-immigrant sentiment was voiced overwhelmingly in conjunction with the topic of welfare reform. During a local neighbourhood forum meeting addressing welfare reform a member of the audience stated that the problem was one of too many immigrants. He exhorted those present to vote for UKIP. Conversations outside the social club, in the smoking area, often mentioned how Black African people, in particular, were reporting under-occupying tenants to the council so that they would be 'kicked out' and the houses given over to them. In this way, neighbourhood rumour, talk and speculation supported and fuelled resentment about immigration and housing (Hewitt 2005). These stories were clearly based on hearsay and speculation, yet there were instances during my fieldwork where the tension arising from such narratives was more directly linked to personal experience and might explain the rising resentment and anger directed towards increasing diversity within the neighbourhood. This is illustrated in the following field diary extract.

FIELD DIARY

3 May 2013

I helped Mary move some of her belongings today. I'd just gone into Mary's house when the door knocked, I asked if she wanted me to get it and when I opened the door there were two Black women standing there with pushchairs and three other small children. The women were dressed in traditional African dress. They asked me if this was the house they'd seen on Homefinder. Mary, coming to the door, said 'I haven't moved out yet'! Mary told the woman to come in anyway and have a look around the house. One of the women came in and Mary showed her around; she said to me 'I feel like an estate agent' and we both laughed. After the woman left we carried on with moving some of the furniture that could fit in my car. Mary seemed a bit quiet after this. I ask her if she was OK and she tells me her hands are hurting her from packing up, she suffers with rheumatoid arthritis. The bungalow is only around the corner so I make a few trips in the car, piling Mary's belongings up in the living room. I leave Mary to it; she looks tired. I tell her I'll be back later on to help.

It appeared that Mary's house had been advertised on the city's social housing website before she had moved out. After this incident had taken place, and after hearing the narratives that were circulating around the neighbourhood, I was left wondering what Mary's response would have been if she had been one of my more angry and vocal participants in terms of their feelings towards minorities. Mary was mixed race, and was one of the few participants who articulated no negative feelings towards increasing diversity within the neighbourhood. The local housing officer with whom I spoke said that he had also experienced anger from tenants and explained how the policy was fuelling resentment:

'It's caused quite a lot of resentment as well. We hear quite a few people say "we don't wanna move out this big house because you'll just stick a family of Africans in it", and as much as we discourage people from talking like that it is their opinion, and erm ... and there's a fair chance it could actually happen as well, erm, so yeah, immigration has had a lot to do with it in my opinion, and managing that is quite difficult because you do get the resentment of "well we've lived round here for years, and you've given my house to a family of Africans" ... Yeah, absolutely, and yeah, we just have to say "well look, you know all our properties go on the city's Homefinder, we don't choose who gets them, you know we haven't just deliberately gone and picked a family from another country to move in just to annoy you" (laughs). People think we do that, erm, have I mentioned that we're building some more houses over SA (another housing estate) over the next couple of years, and already we've had people say "well are they gonna go to local people?" so there is a lot of resentment there about immigration.' (Media housing officer)

There was also evident resentment against the political establishment and a feeling that those in government were far removed, and had no concept about the lives of those who lived in social housing.

'We didn't cause the deficit though!'

In order to understand what sense participants made of the policy, and to explore their subjective understandings of austerity, welfare reform and 'fairness', I posed the question 'why do you think the government introduced the Bedroom Tax?' This question generated responses deeply laden with emotion; it elicited anger, sadness and expressions of morality and injustice. Very few of the participants cited austerity or the budget deficit as a primary reason for its introduction. Mary was one of the few tenants who showed awareness of the intended aims of the policy. She explained that in principle the aims were laudable but that in practice the policy was detrimental to how people lived their lives:

> 'Erm well, they're trying to bring their, erm, their bill down, they're trying to bring the money down, for what they pay out, like the benefit bill and all the rest of it. The money they have to … because I mean, it's colossal it is, and erm, so I mean, I can understand why they're doing it, and I do think it is a good thing why they're doing it, but when they're heaving people from towns and districts and ruining their whole way of life, their whole family network, I mean if you haven't got family, what have you got? It's just gonna be an isolated society, I mean it's just not on.' (Mary)

Jane, a part-time shop assistant, also cited the budget deficit and drew on the discourse of 'we are all in this together'. Jane was willing to do her bit to reduce the deficit by paying for one room, but suggested that paying for two rooms was unreasonable, given the financial constraints that people were under:

Jane: I know you've gotta do your bit for society and society changed over the years and we're in a lot of debt, and to cut the deficit a little bit wouldn't mind paying for one room.

Sid: We didn't cause the deficit though, we didn't say lend loads of money off the Americans, they do it to line their pockets. Half of em have got their tax-free havens where their money goes into …

Jane's boyfriend, Sid, however, argued that the deficit was not caused by them, so why should they be made to pay the price of the government's bad decisions? Jane was dubious about government claims also, because while the government was advocating that people should increase their work hours in order to pay the Bedroom Tax, this was inconsistent with the realities of the job market, as she explained:

> 'What I think's wrong is people that go to work, my point is, people that work like me are trying to fight for hours but if I didn't get them I'm gonna have a really bad time of it. I'm gonna struggle because I'm still gonna have to find 60 quid for the rent, you know what I mean, by the time I hand my wage slips in or whatever, you know what I mean. They go up and I'll have to pay more, which I probably will cus I've had extra hours these last few weeks, it's gonna show. In January, when I've probably got 14 or 15 hours, I'm gonna still have to pay that cus January is a really slack month. Like last year I think I only had nine hours one week, it was bad ...' (Jane)

Jane's employment contract was for seven hours per week, although she was often given extra hours. The problem with this situation was that any increase in hours affected the amount of Housing Benefit she received and the increase would show up on the pay slips she had to present to the Housing Benefit department. In this situation she was at risk of being overpaid Housing Benefit and was penalised if she failed to declare working overtime before the Housing Benefit was paid. Jane desperately wanted to work more hours but they were never guaranteed. This left her in a precarious situation of having to maintain parity with the hours she worked and the amount of Housing Benefit claimed, which had been further reduced because of the Bedroom Tax.

The majority of the participants did not cite austerity as a motivating factor for the introduction of the policy; rather, they suggested, it was a policy that penalised those who claimed benefits:

> 'If this government really wants us to all leave our three-bedroom houses they should have started building one-bedroom flats. You know, they've come up with this cuckoo idea we're gonna chuck em all out, anyone on benefits we're gonna hit everyone ... they don't realise.' (Mick)

'The reason why I think they're doing this to people, I think they're picking on the vulnerable like me, like my friend Mandy, and she's got a disabled husband. They've put her into a doss-hole of a flat (says angrily), they wouldn't give her any money to redecorate, she's had to do it all herself. They were moaning about putting a ramp up because of her husband's mobility scooter, so that took time to do that.' (Emily)

Some felt that the policy targeted the most vulnerable and felt the policy was far from 'fair', enacted by a government that was out of touch with their lives. For many, finding employment that would pay enough so that they would not have to claim Housing Benefit, and thus negate their paying the Bedroom Tax, was untenable. Indeed, even before the implementation of the policy, research was highlighting that the majority of new Housing Benefit claimants were in work (Webb 2012). Being employed does not guard against a reliance on Housing Benefit. Welfare reform is predicated on the idea that it will 'reintroduce the culture of work in households where it may have been absent for generations' (DWP 2010b: 3). This suggestion, that 'welfare dependency' is caused by inter-generational cultures of worklessness, is not supported by empirical evidence; it is a 'great myth' (Shildrick et al 2012: 221). While Jimmy could not work because he was very ill with cancer, his life had been characterised by physical labour, as he explained:

'Well, I was in the car factory for quite a long while and then I was on the buildings for quite a few years ... mainly that, car factories and building sites ... now it takes me all me time to pick a cup of tea up ... these are turning round to people saying "go out get a job, get a job", but there's no jobs out there and the sooner they start thinking about that the better. I'd like one of them MPs to come and live with me and see what I live like, do you know what I mean?' (Jimmy)

The issue of employment was raised, as tenants felt that their unemployed status made them a target for government cuts. Many of the participants spoke about barriers to employment, including ill-health, criminal records and caring responsibilities. They talked of attending Job Centre training courses and their efforts to find employment. The general consensus was that the Job Centre service was inadequate, as Mark was keen to stress:

'I was mainly a construction worker ... now for me to get a construction job around here, I've been on courses, interviews for jobs, but the way the system goes, erm, they say to ya "you need a CSCS [Construction Skills Certification Scheme] card, so go back to the social and let them put you through a course to get a CSCS card". "Right I'll do that", they won't gimme a job till I apply to get a CSCS card. Go to the social and say to them "OK can I do a course so I can get a CSCS card." "Erm yeah, OK, we'll do that if you can get a job." Hold on, I've just been to a job but they said if I can get a CSCS card then they'll give me a job, they just keep passing the buck all the time, even a welding course, one minute I've applied for a welding course – somebody's interested in, like, testing me for a welding course – next thing I know they haven't got the funds to do it. You just keep getting dropped all the time.' (Mark)

While the introduction of the CSCS card scheme has promoted health and safety training for construction workers, it has been criticised on the grounds that it discriminates against construction workers who, if they had started work before the 1980s, had not been required to go to college but are now obliged to gain costly qualifications in order to work. One union secretary stated 'it's a gravy train for the CSCS and upsets a lot of tradesmen who are now missing out on work'.[2] The government was viewed as disconnected, having no insight into the day-to-day realities of how a life on benefits was lived, as the following extracts make clear.

'Cameron, he's alright ain't he, he's alright, when he's retired he'll get chucked out, which I reckon he will. He'll be alright in a nice house and what have ya won't he? He won't go without food, won't go without a roof over his head. It's right though, innit? I wish they'd come round and see how people live, the likes of me and other people, I do, be yourself mate and come round, come round the houses, he'd change his attitude then.' (Jess)

'They need to sit, or they need to survive off the money that we're living off, do exactly what we're doing and they should be given a set amount of time to do it and see how they manage.' (Fiona)

'I think the politicians are liars, they don't give a damn about us working class, the middle class, working class or whatever you wanna call em. They're only in it for themselves, £250 hairstyles, houses that people don't know nothing about, they don't do fuck all. It's like, I think like I keep saying, I think things are gonna go back way, way back to Oliver Twist days for want of a better word, where people are living in shitholes ... I think it's gonna happen.' (Emily)

The main political parties in the UK were seen to give no real political choice, as they appeared to have converged; there was not so much a sense of apathy, more a critical disengagement, reflecting a view that what was on offer politically failed to speak to their interests (Holmes and Manning 2013). Participants spoke about how they had become disengaged and disinterested in politics and, for many, this had resulted in voter abstinence. However, because they felt that they were now at the losing end of government policy, many became politicised and were determined to use their vote:

'Well sometimes I vote, sometimes I don't bother, but now I'll make sure I am voting cus I want these twats out, these bunch of divs. It is, it's gonna be, I've spoke [to neighbour] and me and her were on about it and it's gonna be, your gonna have to have two working families in one place to survive, because when you work it out, I mean you can't put your heating on as much as what you wanna put it on can ya, cus you couldn't afford to keep putting the money into the meter.' (Fiona)

Interviewer: Do you vote, Jess?
Jess: I'm gonna this year, I didn't since I was in me other place but I haven't since, cus I thought they were a load of shite, but this year I'm gonna and my daughter said she will, she said I am as well ... I don't know, I feel like kicking someone's head in (laughs), the government. I felt like writing a letter to him you know, at one stage, I got to the

stage I had it all in my head what I wanted to say
to that what's his name?

Interviewer: Cameron.

Jess: Oh I can't even name him, you know, to say do you realise what you're doing to the likes of people like me ...

Although there was voter apathy among participants, the majority had been Labour supporters in the past and some said they would continue voting Labour as they had vowed to abolish the policy. However, with a lack of political choice and the absence of a mainstream party which they felt represented them, a small minority of participants had decided to vote for UKIP or the BNP, who were seen as defending their interests:

> 'They turned round and Labour said if we get in next time round ... I was sick of voting for them but people are just saying to me I'm voting for UKIP blah, blah, blah. You hear more about UKIP now than Labour from the people I've grown up with, you know.' (Bob)

Others supported the BNP, arguing that while they were viewed as a racist party they were the only party they felt would look after their interests:

Julie: I think it's the government letting em in, but why should we?

Cath: Course it is, you know like, you know the BNP they're seen as a racist party. It ain't, they're just looking out for us, now like we're letting in loads of Kosovos and ...

Julie: It don't matter what they are, they're letting em in.

Cath: Gypsies, they're letting a load of them in now, they just let a load in, our country can just about survive, literally. We are struggling and we're basically giving out handouts ain't we? We have this politics argument all the time so we know all about it but it's just pissing me off. You have to pay more attention to it now, now that this is happening to us.

> 'Well, I always used to be Labour and then the way the country was going I thought I'd go Conservative, but

Conservative are worse than Labour, and then I voted BNP and I thought oh shit I'm gonna get classed as being racist and I'm not, I just want our people and the rights for our people.' (Keith)

The discussion between Cath and her friend Julie highlights how participants felt the mainstream political parties no longer looked after their interests. It also illustrates the perception that immigration had become out of control: 'If the government can no longer look after "us" how can they provide the resources to look after "them"?' was the type of sentiment that was frequently expressed. Cath states that "now this is happening to us" she has to become more politically aware. Her position is lent some weight by evidence from analysis of the 2010 Spending Review which demonstrated that those who did not vote in the 2010 general election faced greater levels of cuts to their annual household income in comparison to those who did vote (Birch et al 2013). Participants struggling to manage cuts in social provision felt that they had to re-engage with politics because their failure to do so had allowed politicians to target cuts at them. Some were drawn towards more right-wing parties because they were the only ones who were seen to represent their interests. Housing was a major factor in this, and the perceived competition for social housing invariably became associated with immigration – a finding that is replicated in other research on white working-class communities (Garner 2011; Beider 2014).

Community integration and housing

New communities have established themselves in the neighbourhood and they make extensive use of the community centre; their children attend the local schools; and they have boosted the congregations of the two local churches. In 2011 the population of Tarley was 84.3% White British. A factsheet on diversity produced by the city council asserts that there is no complete picture of the ethnic composition of the city, but it is diverse compared to the country as a whole. This diversity is reflected in the data obtained from the city's school pupil population, with 44% of pupils being non-White British, while one in three pupils across primary, secondary and special schools speak a language other than English as their first language. It is in such communal places as schools, church and community centre, and in the everyday interactions of the neighbourhood, that people integrate and familiarity is bred. Only in the local social club and pub are minorities observably absent. The local vicar was of the opinion that the neighbourhood had been accepting of new communities:

> 'Erm ... and on the whole I think Tarley has managed that change really well. People, friends of mine, when I moved here, she's from an Asian part of the city and she said "oh Tarley's really racist", "it's just very white working class I wouldn't go in there", and ... but actually that's not my experience at all, those who have come into the area have been welcomed, accepted. I don't think there are that many tensions, erm, they certainly aren't tensions that surface very often, I don't think, so I'm really impressed by that. Erm, so our schools are quite diverse ethnically now ... a good proportion of the congregation are Black Africans. Somehow, I don't know if this is by design or not, but somehow Tarley has more African refugees than other parts of the city I think, or certainly more than from any other community.' (Local vicar)

On an interpersonal level, many of the participants knew and interacted with new communities on a daily basis, as neighbours and as the parents of children who played and went to school together. These participants described them in positive terms, contrary to the negative narratives that were directed at immigration more broadly. Cath said her neighbour was "a darling", while Lisa said how lovely it was that her neighbours would bring round food if they were having a barbeque. Their neighbours' family-orientated values resonated with residents who held close kinship ties in high regard. However, despite the positive interactions participants had on a personal basis, they still questioned the entitlement these neighbours had to their houses over that of British-born people. Positive contact with newcomers did not, therefore, change the opinions participants had about immigration policy or its impact on resources – a finding replicated in other research (Ward 2008). Many ultimately blamed the government for allowing so many immigrants into the country, suggesting that they were the ones at fault rather than immigrants per se.

The sense of loss and anger among those who had downsized appeared magnified when they talked about who had come to occupy the property once they had moved. These tenants would still be in contact with friends, family and former neighbours, which meant they were informed about who the new occupants were. The thought of immigrants being the new occupants caused anger, and appeared to prove their theory correct, that they were being displaced to make room for immigrants. Katie, for example, was bitterly angry about having to move from a home she had occupied for 24 years. The following interview extract shows her rising anger as she talks about those who now occupy her former home.

Katie:	(whispers something)
Interviewer:	Say that again?
Katie:	(laughs) I can't say that.
Interviewer:	Be absolutely honest, I want your honest opinion about things.
Katie:	Soon as I moved out, black people moved in. I knew that's what was gonna happen.
Daughter:	After they decorated the whole bloody house first as well.
Katie:	(voice rises) So how come English people can't get all the luxuries what they're getting?
Interviewer:	Were they African or English?
Katie:	They were African.
Daughter:	No they were jamoggies, like Jamaican … big.
Interviewer:	Were they from England, though?
Katie:	I wouldn't say they were, I wouldn't say they'd grown up in England …
Interviewer:	How does that make you feel?
Katie:	Horrible.
Friend:	Fred [former neighbour] felt horrible as well didn't he?
Katie:	Yeah, the neighbours don't like em.
Interviewer:	So what were you saying about the government bringing it in, you think immigrants get treated better?
Katie:	Yeah they are, they get shop vouchers, they get new cars, everything (voice rises). What do we get? Jack shit! Apart from being thrown into a dump of a bleeding flat and they take my house. Oh I am annoyed, yeah, I'm well pissed off with it actually …

Katie, a white occupant, makes a racial distinction when prompted about whether or not the new occupants are English; she gives no firm answer because she does not actually know. For Katie, the fact that the occupants are black is enough to convince her that 'indigenous' local residents are losing out to immigrants. Katie also makes reference to what immigrants are entitled to: shop vouchers and new cars. Such stories were commonplace among participants; these newcomers were being giving help, it seemed, with everything, while at the same time their own entitlement to benefits was being assessed and their homes were under threat. At the time I interviewed Bob, a new street of housing had been built directly behind his street. During the interview Bob urged me to go upstairs and look out of the back bedroom window so that I could see for myself that the street had been entirely populated by Black African families. Moreover, he stated that these homes had been carpeted and satellite dishes erected for the new occupants before they had even moved in. These stories give added emphasis to the perception that newcomers are being advantaged in all areas, at the expense of local residents.

What lies at the heart of participants' feelings and expressions of anger and resentment is a sense of loss and abandonment – themes that have emerged in other work relating to the white working class and housing (Dench et al 2006; Garner 2009; Garner 2010; Beider 2012). Much of this work, however, was done before the Welfare Reform Act 2012 had begun to impact on people. Before this, research shows that, particularly on estates and in relation to social housing, there was already resentment about the impact of immigration and the perceived competition over social housing. Further, as Ward (2008) noted, the availability of social housing is greater on poorer social housing estates, and as a consequence it is these neighbourhoods which have disproportionately absorbed economically disadvantaged migrants and refugees. This has raised questions about the impact of immigration on community relations and service provision – questions which have not been adequately addressed as to how these processes are being experienced by both economically disadvantaged immigrants and receiving populations (Robinson and Reeve 2006; Robinson 2008; Phillips et al 2010). Add to this situation a policy that is perceived as forced movement and eviction, and tensions rise even higher. For those who face losing their homes because of the Bedroom Tax, these fears become heightened and magnified; they make a direct correlation: 'we' get 'kicked out', migrants move in. However, as Bottero (2009: 7) argues, fixating on 'whiteness' or ethnicity 'sidesteps the real issue of class inequality, focusing on how disadvantaged groups compete for scarce resources, rather than exploring how that scarcity is shaped in the first place'. The real issue here is the scarcity of social housing; it is not just about who gets allocated it, but who gets to keep a stake in it as welfare state restructuring begins to impact on people's lives. Amin (2002: 6) argues that social deprivation heightens ethnic resentment and difference because it removes 'part of the material wellbeing and social worth that can help in reducing jealousy and aggression towards others seen to be competing for the same resources'. Indeed, two of the participants blamed the government for fuelling the resentment they felt towards immigrants:

> 'When I was young I was very racist towards foreigners, very, but as time went on I changed, but now the government are making me more racist cus they're treating them better than their own.' (Keith)

Emily: I've never been prejudiced, but I'm really getting there and it isn't my fault, it's the government's fault for bringing them over.

Interviewer: So have you felt more like that since the Bedroom Tax?

Emily: Oh yeah, because as far as I'm concerned they want me out of here so they can put them in here, and I know I shouldn't feel like, but I am, I am. But if I said anything out there I'd get done for it, it's not called England anymore.

The Tarley neighbourhood has seen an increase in new communities in recent decades, and while that may have served to make the area more diverse, long-standing social tenants were not directly in competition with newcomers for social housing because they were already housed. However, the housing insecurity engendered by the Bedroom Tax, and the process of downsizing and rejoining social housing waiting lists, has served to increase the perception of competition for housing, fuelling tensions that were already present and creating new ones. While I was waiting in court with Cath and her children's father to be called in about their notice seeking possession, Cath's former partner was railing against the government. Pacing about, he stopped and looked at me, saying "we're sitting on a pressure cooker and eventually it's gonna blow". I asked him what he was referring to: "immigration", he said.

Conclusion

Historically, housing was and remains a highly emotive issue but there are other factors at play here. The working class has always been internally divided, characterised by distinctions between the rough and the respectable. In recent times, damaging representations of those who live in social housing and who claim benefits have become endemic. The participants in this study feel the effects of this stigmatisation both from wider society and from people within their own community. These discourses are diffused throughout the working class and people react in opposition to them, characterising others using the same language as a way to reclaim their own sense of value and worth. These divisions in and between the working class, fostered by the notion of the worker and the shirker, undermine solidarity. The common cause is obfuscated as, any serious discussion about housing and the increasingly dire state of need for accessible, low cost-housing and people's ability to gain access to it, is ignored. The Bedroom Tax not only increased material deprivation, it positioned participants as unworthy of their homes because of so-called 'welfare dependency'. Moreover, in order to downsize, tenants had to rejoin social housing waiting lists, which brought into sharper focus the dearth of smaller properties and the massive demand for social housing. Taken together, these factors heighten the feeling of being in competition for housing, resulting in greater animosity towards perceived 'others'. To implement a policy that further undermines housing stability, when research has shown it to be an already emotive and contentious issue of primary concern, has worked to heighten and create more division and resentment.

6

Community and belonging

In Chapter 5 it was demonstrated how the importance of housing, and the perceived competition for it, was exacerbated by the Bedroom Tax and generated heightened resentment about immigration. Another strong theme to emerge from this study was the importance of community and being able to maintain housing within the neighbourhood. This throws up questions about notions of 'community' and place attachment. What forms the basis of attachment to a geographical area? Is it place itself, or the social bonds that have formed in that place, which engenders feelings of emotional attachment and belonging? Research on the Bedroom Tax has highlighted that an unwillingness to move from the local area is an important driver in determining why those affected by the policy have been reluctant to downsize (Bragg et al 2015). Locality clearly matters, but, empirically, what can the imposition of the Bedroom Tax tell us about why it matters, and to whom? What can the Bedroom Tax tell us about working-class residents' attachment to their community in the light of possible displacement? Does it undercut feelings of local attachment and belonging? Or does it serve to reinforce them? Mulligan (2015) notes the historical and contemporary 'deep ambivalence' about the concept of community, not least because there is little agreement among sociologists about what community actually is. This chapter explores the different ways in which people and place are tied together, in order to understand the role of community (real or imagined) in its full complexity.

In studies of neighbourhoods that are disadvantaged, a key concern has been the high turnover of residents, which can work to inhibit the development of community commitment (Barke and Turnbull 1992; Power 1997; Venkatesh 2008). Implicit in this assertion is that community commitment, or attachment, is fostered by longevity within a neighbourhood and the establishment of trust and social bonds that transience would undermine. Notions of community, it has been suggested, 'have questions of belonging at their centre' (Mooney and Neal 2009: 94). This raises the question about who is seen to belong and who does not. As demonstrated by this study, while the word 'community' has positive connotations of shared values, comfort and warmth, it also has a dark side, working to exclude as well as include (Mooney and Neal 2009).

Clinging on to community

'Erm, I worked in H [another estate in the city] before here, so I would say H and Tarley are similar in the sense that there are a lot of people struggling with some of the tough stuff in life. So both communities, you've got a lot of social housing, you've got a lot of people who are on benefits and then the knock-on effect of all that, so quite a lot of poverty ... quite a lot of, erm, long-term health issues, mental health issues, and addiction problems. So there are similarities between the communities ... For me the differences are, obviously H is very ethnically diverse and I don't think has such a strong sense of "we are one community". Tarley feels to me almost like a village within a city because there is a sense of Tarley identity that people have, helped by the fact that there's a sort of centre and helped by the fact that we're almost cut off by the A road and the railway line, so there is this local identity isn't there? Like people know when you're in Tarley, erm ... and I think that's really good, that sense of Tarley community and community spirit is brilliant, erm. Tarley I think has changed a bit in the ten years I've been here, in the sense it's become more ethnically diverse than it used to be. I don't know if you would agree with that ...' (Local vicar)

This extract underscores the idea that there is within Tarley a strong sense of local identity. The estate, positioned as it is on the outskirts of the city, may indeed, as the vicar suggests, have helped in forging this identity. Further, if we look to the history of the estate, the 'old precinct', as it is often referred to by residents, with nostalgia, formed the centre of Tarley, and provided such an array of different shopping outlets that there was very little need to travel into the city centre. Three pubs and a social club also helped to facilitate social interaction between the residents of the estate. In the late 1970s and 1980s the city's manufacturing base began to decline rapidly, which led to the loss of many well-paid factory jobs. These changes had a dramatic impact in Tarley and, over the years, the neighbourhood became economically and socially isolated from the rest of the city. However, research conducted in Tarley as part of a project looking at the city's 'priority neighbourhoods' suggested that the area benefited from both a strong sense of community and a strong community identity. Similarly, research conducted on the St Ann's estate in

Nottingham by Mckenzie (2015: 47) noted how respondents talked of 'being St Ann's'; belonging to the estate mattered and was bound up with cultural and social meanings, about being known, fitting in and feeling respected. This sense of belonging was important in light of how Mckenzie's respondents felt they were 'looked down on and excluded outside of the estate' (Mckenzie 2015: 75). This replicates the sense of belonging to the estate that is found among the participants in this study. Fried (2000: 194) noted that 'despite the widespread usage of terms like community or place attachment, there has been little explicit attention to the psychosocial dynamics of attachment behaviour'. Such attachments to place can be multidimensional. The tenants in this study had lived the majority, or all, of their lives on the estate and had built close friendship ties. As Don explained, nearly all respondents had close family and kin living within the area:

> 'All of em, all around are my family and friends; as I say, I was born five doors up. John owns that house because my mum passed away. Jill lives two doors up that way. My brother lives in the block of flats just over there and my other brother lives in the first street there. And another one lives round the corner up there.' (Don)

Research has shown that 'no matter the operationalisation of the construct, length of residence has remained a strong predictor of community attachment with few exceptions' (Trentelman 2009: 202). This research supports this assertion, as long-standing estate residents articulated a sense of attachment to the local area. This attachment was bound up with social relationships, and it was longevity of residence on the estate that had enabled participants to build up local social networks. Close family connections are invaluable within the informal caring economy; grandparents helped to look after grandchildren and adults looked out for their parents. Such informal caring practices were not confined to family members, however, as Mo explained when she spoke about taking in "waifs and strays":

Mo: Three bedroom, yeah, two girls, three boys. But I've also had everyone else's kids, you know I brought up Karen and all, cus she was going into care, and so we had her till she left school and then she moved in with Billy. But we'd always had lodgers, do you know what I mean? There was always someone living here, you know. We were never on our own for long. As soon as someone moved out ... Kenny, when he lost his mum and dad we had him for, oh God years, years he lived here, there was always someone that needed somewhere to live, so we put em up (laughs).

Interviewer: Half-way house (laughing).

Mo: Oh yeah, more than that (laughing), we used to get all the waifs and strays, you know. The lads as they were growing up, all their mates and even my lad had left home and the mate was still coming here.

Close local connections gave participants a sense of security, particularly when they were dealing with the issues in their lives. The Bedroom Tax posed a threat to maintaining social support systems that helped participants cope with ill-health, for example, because they did not know where they might be rehoused. Nadine had undergone an operation to remove a brain tumour, which had left her with epilepsy and at times debilitating depression. Discussing an attempt to swap houses with someone in the neighbourhood, she explained why living close to her daughters and being able to rely on friends, no matter what the time of day or night, was vital:

'It's my community, it's everything, and I said to him [housing officer] as well, I says, I know it's gonna be a hard job, cus I knew erm, I thought I'd try Hannah again but I didn't have much hope anyway, and erm, as I said, Macey lives two minutes up there, Chloe lives just by the rent office ... It's the area, I know it's a dump and all the rest of it, but ... We, who've been here, and we have got a community, I know for a fact I could knock on my friend's door at two in the morning and she'd look after me.' (Nadine)

Community, for Nadine, was having family or friends living nearby whom she could call on for help in difficult times. For Nadine, downsizing was not just about moving or swapping houses, it could potentially mean that she would have to move out of the estate and away from her social support networks. Yuval-Davis et al (2005: 526) assert that 'a notion of belonging becomes activated when there is a sense of exclusion'. It may well be the case that the potential loss of a home and community activated a deeper sense of belonging to the neighbourhood; it brought into sharper focus what could be lost.

The idea of community also had more tangible benefits, with some participants suggesting that local people pulled together when tragedy struck. Two of the three pubs had been closed down in Tarley, but the local social club still provided a space for people to socialise. During the week, the club is mostly occupied by older men, playing dominoes or watching sport, but on a Sunday afternoon the concert room is filled almost to capacity with people playing bingo, hoping to win some money. What the club provides is an invaluable space for social interaction; it is a local space that stands at the heart of the neighbourhood, negating the need to travel. Being a member of the club means that a function room can be hired for the price of a small, refundable deposit, and birthdays and funerals are celebrated and mourned there. Further, and in an era where funeral costs are expensive, if someone needed help to meet these costs a collection would be conducted in the concert hall on a Sunday when the club was at its busiest. These collections would raise hundreds of pounds, just from people throwing in £1 or more. During the course of fieldwork, Jess's sister and mother died within a few weeks of each other. Their funeral costs were covered, in part, by the contributions of people in the local area. These sources of support are invaluable for people who are trying to bury their dead on a low income. It was through such gestures of 'community spirit' that participants came to value their neighbourhood, as Katie and her daughter made clear:

Interviewer:	Can you describe the area for me?
Katie:	I love it, cus everybody comes together when summat goes wrong, as you know, tragedies and things like that... it's a close-knit family, ain't it really?
Daughter:	It might be a shithole but it's like it's our shithole, I mean it's our home big time.
Katie:	I don't think I could ever move out of Tarley.

Neighbourhood institutions such as social clubs are grassroots organisations that provide leisure and social interaction and, despite their ongoing demise, still stand at the heart of many working-class communities. Ruth Cherrington (2012: xix), who has documented the social history of working men's clubs, asserts that these social spaces mean more than 'just beer and bingo'. As she states, 'the need for people to "club together" for pleasure, mutual support and practical help is perhaps even more vital today than ever before'. The club owed its very existence to the fact that early neighbourhood residents had raised the funds to help build it. Research has shown that reduced resources due to the Bedroom Tax have impacted on social relationships and interaction, leading to greater social isolation (Moffatt et al 2015). This has been the case also for some of the participants in this study who could no longer afford to socialise in the club. This has led to greater social isolation and depression, and could have a knock-on effect on the club, which relies on the patronage of local people for its survival.

This is not to deny or overlook the social problems of the neighbourhood. One of the local pubs suffered a certain notoriety before it was bulldozed, and there are issues of youth violence and drugs. This estate had always had its social problems and, the vicar states, still does:

> 'Yeah, yeah, and it's one of the big things people talk about … people kind of fear some of the young groups that hang around outside the library. Some of that's just about perception, but there is a bit of a gang culture around and that draws some of the young people into stuff they shouldn't be involved in.' (Local vicar)

Despite the neighbourhood having been given a makeover, insofar as Media Housing Association had re-rendered many of the 'no fines' blocks of flats and houses, and landscaped the area, there was the perception that some parts of the neighbourhood were in decline. Burglaries from homes, cars and vans appeared to be on the increase, while local community support officers had been disbanded and formal policing in the area had declined. Some parts of the neighbourhood, particularly the early Radburn-layout housing, were seen as 'rougher' than others parts, as Ruby made clear:

Ruby: It's like Beirut up here now and that used to be, you know, like the nicer bit. That one Lyn had, I don't know whether there's gypos or what in it – you know, where you cut through, Lyn had it, that house on its own, fucking dirty nappies, everything threw in the front garden, in the entry. It's just minging round here now compared with what it used to be. I mean the kids, like Luke when he was younger, he was too scared to go over the park cus

	of all the big ones, all the teenagers sitting there, if he went to the park I'd have to go with him. It has gone, I think it's gone right down compared to what it was.
Jay:	It's that old scenario isn't it, 30 years ago you could leave your back door open … they tore the old precinct down and they ripped the heart out of Tarley.
Ruby:	Yeah. Definitely.
Jay:	That changed things didn't it?
Interviewer:	Why did they knock it down?
Jay:	I don't know why they didn't just put the same sort of shops back and build it without the flats and things, the butcher, the baker and the candlestick maker, you know.
Ruby:	It was brilliant years ago, they had everything; you didn't need to go to town really.
Jay:	They sold it to the ones that built the houses and bought them out cus the Co-op bought the land or something, or they owned a lot of the land because they owned the top half of the precinct and the bottom half was basically sold off for development, wasn't it?

Community here is invoked as imagined, viewed in terms of safety and security but seen to have declined with the regeneration of the estate and the demolition of the main shopping area. The social problems of the estate are highlighted and directed at the young people who 'hang around' and people who didn't look after the area. Despite the social problems of the neighbourhood there was the opinion that other estates suffered similar problems. However, longevity on the estate, and development of family connections and social networks, meant that many participants knew from where and from whom such problems stemmed. Regardless of Ruby's assertions about the decline of the area, her reaction when asked how she would feel if she had to move out of Tarley was one of defiance that she was determined to stay. The next section details the reaction of participants when they spoke about the possibility of being displaced from Tarley and shows that, despite the problems of the neighbourhood, tenants still preferred to remain living there. This is especially true of older participants and those who relied upon the support of relatives and friends living close by. For those participants who were working or studying, relocation was less of an issue. They worked outside of the estate and some had their own transport, which meant they could still call upon the networks of support they needed, such as help with childcare. For them, moving out of the neighbourhood represented social mobility if their economic circumstances improved enough. However, given the choice between remaining in social housing and staying in a neighbourhood they knew, or moving to another estate, they too preferred to stay where they were. Living in social housing in Tarley was preferable to being relocated to other estates with high levels of social housing and similar social problems. The lack of smaller properties available locally meant that, for participants in this study, the introduction of the Bedroom Tax created real anxiety that they might have to relocate outside of the neighbourhood.

Fear of displacement: the ties that bind

In the preceding chapters it was shown how tenants struggled to remain living in their homes despite falling into debt and fuel and food poverty. When their financial situations became untenable they did look to downsize. At last contact, seven of the participants in this study had downsized to smaller properties within the neighbourhood. Mary was very lucky to have been offered a one-bedroom property around the corner from her previous home. Shelley was also able to downsize to a property a few streets away from her old home. The process of moving was traumatic, but paled into insignificance when contrasted with being displaced from the neighbourhood, as Mary explained:

'Oh I mean, I'd have hated it, I'd, I'd, even though I wasn't really in a position to, but I think I would have refused it. Because I, I mean even in my own neighbourhood where I know everybody, everybody knows me, I sometimes feel isolated, because I ain't got any money to go out. You can't just go for a walk. If you got no money what's the point of just walking, you know and when you're feeling … I'm not disabled, but I'm getting on in years and I find it hard to walk … blah, blah, blah. Yeah, you're isolated, I would have actually hated it. I mean, my daughter moved back into Tarley, which she hated for years, just to be near me. And so if they had to move me back out of Tarley it would have been catastrophic, oh you know, horrendous. I would have refused it, which wouldn't have been a very good move, so I really been lucky to get a place just round the corner. I've only moved about 400 yards in the last 40-odd years (laughing).' (Mary)

Such was the fear of being displaced, Mary said, that she would have refused to move if it had meant moving out of Tarley, which could have resulted in her accumulating greater levels of rent arrears. For her, displacement would have been "catastrophic". The support she received from her daughter and the threat of being separated spatially from the people and place she had spent so many years living in represented further isolation; her whole structure of attachments would have been under threat. For Jessica and Katie the fear of displacement was such that they had accepted properties in other parts of the neighbourhood that they were unhappy with. For them, anything was better than being relocated away from family and friends. Katie articulates the lengths she would have gone to in order to avoid displacement:

'I wouldn't have liked it, I wouldn't have moved out the area, I wouldn't have, no. I'd have barricaded meself in that house. I wouldn't have moved out the area. I think it was disgusting how they treated me in the first place anyway; cus I was giving up a perfectly good three-bedroom house.' (Katie)

These three tenants had physical problems and relied heavily on the support of family who lived close by to help out with practical needs such as shopping and household chores. However, the proximity of friends and family provided psychological support also, which was of particular relevance for those who, because of mobility problems, spent a lot of time in their homes. These tenants in time adapted to their new homes, as Marris (1974: 57) has observed in his study of slum-clearing displacements: 'if the new home is adaptable to their way of life, the adjustment is soon made – the old patterns of shopping, meeting, visiting find their counterpart in new spaces'. For others, the potential effects of displacement were seen as being so traumatic that it could possibly be detrimental to their health, as Billy explained:

'It would be worse, especially my wife, she wouldn't wanna move out this area. This is what my argument always has been. Oh yeah, they offer you somewhere or they find you a nice property, it's supposed to be your own choice, and all of a sudden we've found you a nice property in another part of the city but you don't wanna go there do you. Jenny has lived, Jenny herself, yeah, has lived here for 50 years, lived in Tarley all her life, so I can see her being really ill, if it happens Kelly. Yeah, I think it will affect her that bad ... I wouldn't like to think how bad to be honest with you.' (Billy)

Nadine, who was able to downsize to another property by doing a mutual exchange with a family living across the road, also stated that displacement would have had severe psychological repercussions for her:

'Oh God, I don't think I could've coped. I couldn't have, no. No, that would have destroyed me, I would have probably ended up in the Quins [mental health hospital]. That – that for me would have been, nah, just devastating.' (Nadine)

These tenants were willing, out of financial necessity, to move from their homes, but displacement out of the neighbourhood was inconceivable. They had no wish to move in the first instance and felt that they were ultimately being 'forced' out of their homes. To face the prospect of being 'forced' out of their community as well was something they would not contemplate. Studies which have focused on displacement brought about by slum clearance have documented the psychological impact that displacement has, which, it has been argued, is analogous to feelings of bereavement and grief (Fried 1966; Marris 1974).

For tenants who had children, displacement could mean moving school and losing friends. They wanted to protect their children from the prospect of having to relocate, as Ruby made clear:

'I wouldn't, I wouldn't like it, I wouldn't like it at all, I wouldn't, I definitely wouldn't move out the area, cus I wouldn't know anybody, my babby wouldn't, my babby, I know he's 14, but he wouldn't know anyone, he'd have to go to a new school ... I don't think it's right moving me out the area anyway, when we've lived here all our lives, do you know ...' (Ruby)

The same issues concerned Teresa. She felt her daughters were safe in a neighbourhood where they were known and, as for Ruby, moving could have meant the children having to move school. Moreover, displacement would mean splitting up her family, as her older daughter resided with her grandmother in a flat across the road:

'I moved back to Tarley when I was 18. I got my first flat around the corner. It didn't go too well in there so I kind of moved on and moved back here in '97, beginning of '98, and I've been here ever since, and I'd actually rather be round here than anywhere because I know for a fact if one of my kids go missing I know there's a hundred people round here, whether they know me or not, they know my girls which ... But in other areas you wouldn't get it, I mean, it's different. It's not like oh my God it's the best community, but it pretty much is. Like I say, I'd rather be here than anywhere at the minute, especially till my kids are older. And they're getting there fast (laughs) ... I would be devastated ... as would the girls, because they've been here all their lives, this is what they know, so it would be devastating especially ... Chances are, if I had to move it would split the family completely because I'd have to leave her over there because for the first couple of years me thinking she was coming back, although we all work as one household anyway.' (Teresa)

The informal caring economy and women's mutual support networks and caring responsibilities were important at the level of community. Home may provide ontological security, but the neighbourhood provided 'ontological anchorage' (Hage 2004) in lives where relationships were interconnected. The higher concentration of female-headed households in social housing is due in part to housing allocation policies that prioritise housing on the basis of need, 'but it also reflects the difficulties faced by women on their own in trying to secure and sustain access to housing elsewhere' (Wasoff 1998: 131). Single parents have been incentivised to work via workfare policies and cuts to Housing Benefit. However, in order that they can work they have to make provision for their caring responsibilities and it is often the immediate locality and informal welfare provided by friends and family that makes work possible. For single parents with children, moving in order to maximise employment opportunity made little sense. They did not have the funds to move and did not want to relocate away from the support networks that made work feasible.

Participants' attachment to their neighbourhood was, then, multidimensional. Practically and psychologically, having the support of kinship and friendship networks were key reasons why participants wanted to remain within the neighbourhood. Single mothers such as Teresa and Ruby were able to cope with the multiple problems of mental health issues and raising children because they had family support around them. The effects of displacement have been studied in the context of slum clearance; as Tom Slater (2013: 6) notes, such studies were set in a different time and place, under a different set of circumstances, but for those who have been affected by the Bedroom Tax 'the grieving for lost homes (and communities) comes across just as intensely'. I would suggest further that the displacement from homes and communities is not the same as being displaced because of the destruction of a neighbourhood; these participants' homes and their community are still standing and, as was discussed in Chapter 5, some former tenants believe that their old properties are being reallocated to new migrant communities. This adds a different dimension, because such a belief creates resentment, a feeling that their place in their community is being undermined by others who are seen as having less entitlement because they are newcomers. Delanty (2010) asserts that the contemporary condition of flexible labour, and the failure associated with not being able to make something of yourself within the labour market, leads people to search for a sense of depth and attachment in other areas of their lives. Thus, he asserts, 'the "we" is a protective strategy. The desire for community is largely defensive and, for that reason, can easily take authoritarian forms, as in the rejection of immigrants and other perceived outsiders' (Delanty 2010: 51). As discussed in the previous chapter, as participants' positions within 'their' neighbourhood came under threat, they began to draw boundaries about who has the right to belong and who does not. To resist the feeling that they are becoming excluded, tenants draw more heavily on the notion of 'community', 'their' community, because, as they struggle to pay the Bedroom Tax and as arrears are accumulated, they live with the fear that one day they may be displaced. Community becomes more important to them precisely because there is a fear that it may be taken away.

Many of the tenants spoke about how the neighbourhood was becoming increasingly ethnically diverse; a Polish shop had been opened in the precinct and the schools were said to be full of 'foreigners'. More pervasive was the feeling that "you don't know your neighbours" (Eric). The following extracts illustrate some of the sentiments expressed.

'This fucking area's changed completely. Look at the school, Catholic school 72% is it, 72 or 78% of the pupils in there are immigrants. There's your statistics there, there you go, that's a big one ain't it ... put that in your pipe and smoke it girl ... and it's the truth.' (Bob)

'In the street I think there's just the four families, they're all Polish or African, everyone who used to live in this street, well in the last ten years it changed, the only people that was here originally was like my mum, me, Allan and Kim round the corner. People move in and move out. Before no one did that did they? And you see all the people that have lived in their houses for years and now having to move out and downsize, and that ain't right cus they can't afford to keep up with the Bedroom Tax.' (Cath)

'This is gonna sound really racist, you know, like when you go to the school, they're not like, there's not one person that speaks English, they're all like Polish and that, and our kids are trying to get into the school but they've took over it cus they're Catholics, [I'm] telling you, go down there. Now Sophie, all the kids that have been at that school all these years, and they're saying Sophie hasn't got a place at the nursery, and do you know, like next year, she might get a place in the end, but then it comes to reception, you know, your academic year, there ain't no definite guarantees she'll get one of them either.' (Cath)

Despite the fact that Tarley is still a majority white neighbourhood, the feeling of being 'swamped' by migrants was such that Louise felt that white residents had become the minority, as she explained:

'I've seen the neighbourhood evolve over the years ... it's gone from being, erm, a very monoracial area where it was quite scary to be a black child ... to being quite a multicultural area, where I think, erm, the minority is erm, is white people. And I think they feel awkward and uncomfortable with the fact that they are a minority.' (Louise)

New communities in Tarley are visible because the area had for so long been overwhelmingly white. However, I would suggest that because tenants felt they were being 'forced' out to accommodate 'immigrants', their eyes were drawn to their presence in a way they had not been before. They were searching for the evidence to justify existing convictions. As Harper Lee observed in the classic novel *To Kill a Mockingbird* (1974: 177), 'people generally see what they look for, and hear what they listen for'.

Wacquant (2008: 1) asserts that advanced marginality involves the abandonment of people to 'territories of relegation'. Indeed, advanced marginality is a threat to these tenants. If they lose their homes and the social networks they rely on, they are not being relegated, they are, they feel, being expelled. Slater (2013: 8) argues that 'it is not overstating the case to summarise contemporary welfare and housing policy in Britain as: *the displacement and financial ruin of the poor*'. Neighbourhoods such as Tarley and the social housing tenants that live in them know that they are territorially stigmatised because they live in social housing and because they claim rent support. This has been used as justification not just to make better use of social housing but to incentivise work. What it is effectively doing, however, is threatening 'to drive them out of a coveted space' (Wacquant 2008: 240). This is what Wacquant refers to as the 'loss of hinterland'. He states: 'in previous phases of modern capitalism crises and restructuring, workers temporarily rejected from the labour market could fall back upon the social economy of their community of provenance' (Wacquant 2008: 243). In the case of Tarley, this was facilitated by the longevity of residents. Particularly for the vulnerable people in this study, there is a strong desire to remain 'fixed' in place in 'financially and ontologically insecure times' (Paton 2013: 84). As Tyler (2015: 12) found in her research, 'what many disenfranchised people actually desire is not *flight* but rather *anchorage*'. These tenants do not fear 'relegation to decaying neighbourhoods' (Wacquant 2008), they fear re-relegation to neighbourhoods where they may be isolated, lonely and their needs unmet. Participants were aware of the housing shortage within the neighbourhood and a local housing officer made clear the high demand, stating: "when you go on Homefinder even our flats which are in a big block, which maybe isn't the nicest, will still get over a hundred people bidding on it".

Place attachment reinforces the desire to remain within the neighbourhood. From a policy perspective it has been noted that a high turnover of residents within neighbourhoods can be detrimental to promoting stability, social networks and cohesion (Livingston et al 2008). We have been through a period in which phrases such as 'community cohesion', 'community regeneration' and, more recently, the Conservatives' 'Big Society' agenda all aim at fostering community empowerment and civic duty. Yet in the context of the introduction of a policy that seemingly works to displace people from their communities and which stokes ethnic tension, such concepts and ideology appear worthless. The drive to further privatise social housing and force out long-term residents will work in the opposite direction by weakening the bonds and social networks of support that are vital to the wellbeing of some of our most vulnerable people. Participants' place attachment was inextricably linked to social connections and familial networks that operated *in place*. One participant concluded that what the government was effectively doing to people was "breaking em up, splitting them up and sending them here, there and everywhere" (Jay). While it may be the case, sociologically speaking, that 'the vagueness of definition of "community" and its surrogates are notorious' (Procter 1990: 160), politically, the term becomes just as ambiguous, as Hancock et al make clear:

> Just as the previous New Labour government relied on the labile qualities of community to pursue its neoliberalizing agenda, the current UK Coalition government uses community to define and frame both the broken society and the big, caring, mutual and self reliant society to secure its intensification. (Hancock et al 2012: 347)

Communities are at one and the same time deemed 'broken' and yet seen to be responsible for fixing themselves by fostering mutual responsibility and self-help. Paradoxically, the Bedroom Tax policy appeared to work against this goal of fostering a big, caring society. Putting aside the concepts of community and the debate about whether communities are 'imagined', 'grounded' or 'projected' (Mulligan 2015), empirically, community matters. It is precisely because participants had a long history of living on the estate that they felt that they were part of a community. Indeed, it has been suggested that 'relationships between neighbours on any housing estate develop slowly as trust is established and they learn to do small things for each other ... key [people] are among those who leave ... transience strikes right at the foundations of community (SUSS Centre, quoted in Power 1997: 245).

The participants in this study were not a mobile population; economically they could not afford to live in private rented accommodation or buy a home. Added to this, the dearth of social housing meant that their housing options were limited. In the face of the economic downturn and austerity measures participants did not want the further destabilisation that displacement might bring. Bragg et al (2015: 88) highlighted in their research 'the intrinsic connections between material, social and psychological conditions that link home, neighbourhood, school and community'. The concept of 'community' is contested, debated, deemed obsolete or harnessed for political rhetoric. Meanwhile, for those whose 'communities' are spoken and written about and used to justify state policies, their community may represent the last bastion of defence against a state that they feel wants to stigmatise, penalise and cast them asunder. The policy treats homes in isolation, taking no consideration of the interconnectedness of people's lives and how they are lived within neighbourhoods. Tenants feel under threat from newcomers because their own position within the neighbourhood is threatened. Community thus has a dark side, used as justification to exclude others who are 'new' to the area and seen as less entitled to belong.

Participants' fear of being displaced from the neighbourhood was also tied to how they envisaged the future for themselves and their families. Many participants spoke in broadly negative terms about their future prospects. Things just seemed to be getting progressively worse. The old certainties that had enabled participants to remain within the neighbourhood, put down roots and build localised relationships were seen as under threat. Labour market uncertainty and deindustrialisation had been mitigated to a certain extent by the stability afforded by social housing and Housing Benefit. Cuts in the form of the Bedroom Tax signalled the terminal decline of the welfare state, which could no longer be relied upon:

'The only people who's gonna survive or what's it is people who are rich and the ones who's gonna get, and the people are gonna get poorer and poorer in months to come, and what's gonna happen if the government and the council get their way? By the time I'm 65 they reckon you won't even be entitled to a pension.' (Billy)

'I'm struggling, I'm just about keeping my head above water. It's made me feel ten times worse in myself, I'm more depressed, I'm more worried about my children and my grandchild; you know, what the future holds for them. I am, yeah ...' (Bob)

While Mo joked about ending up homeless, this was an all too real possibility. She had witnessed others become homeless because of their inability to adapt to the Bedroom Tax, and her own position was precarious as she was in rent arrears. Mo envisaged a drastically reduced welfare state in which benefit payments would no longer be available:

'Oh, I don't see no future really, I just see me living in cardboard boxes over the field (laughing). Mind you – couldn't even go into an old people's home could you, cus it would cost you (laughing). I don't see no future really, there ain't none now is there? Mind you, it might be because of my age – ain't much future left; but even for the kids, I think oh, cus God knows what's gonna be happening to them when they're this age – well, not my age even, left school. What it's gonna be like? But I think that's why they're stopping all the social and that by then. That's why they give that money, the kids when they were born all got 200 pound didn't they, and it's to be kept till they're 18, and really you know, all the what do you call it, interest, builds up. That is cus there ain't gonna be no social then. There ain't, no, that's to keep you going till you get a job, till you go to college or whatever.' (Mo)

There was a feeling that worse was to come; as Don stated, "this government are worse than ever, and it's gonna get worse as well".

Wacquant's (2009) assertion that welfare reform in the US was both material and symbolic has resonance here with how the participants in this study felt about welfare state restructuring in the UK. Symbolically, Wacquant argued, reform in the US aimed both to reshape subjectivities into accepting reduced and time-limited welfare and to lower people's expectations about what the state will and should provide. Participants' experience of the Bedroom Tax, as well as other reforms that involved reassessment of claims, tougher sanctioning and denial of eligibility, in contradiction of what their own doctors had stated about their health status, represented a direction of travel that would see the system dismantled. For Wacquant, the conversion of welfare into workfare 'is *not* a mechanical response to economic changes so much as an *exercise in state crafting* aimed at producing – and then adapting to – these very changes' (Wacquant 2009: 103; Lorey 2015). In the UK context, welfare reform, and in particular the Bedroom Tax, was not just aimed at making better use of social housing. Housing Benefit reforms, stated Iain Duncan Smith, should have 'a transformative effect on the lives of those who in the past were faced with a system which trapped people into cycles of worklessness and dependency' (cited in *The Independent* 2015).

One of the stated aims of the Bedroom Tax is to incentivise work, and it can be viewed as a form of workfare in itself. As Peck (2001) suggests, 'workfare' is a generic term that can be applied to a whole range of policies that have within them a welfare-to-work component. Despite the assertion that the Bedroom Tax would help to lower spending on Housing Benefit, in 2015–16 it was £1 billion higher than in 2010–11 (Joyce 2015). If the policy has failed in its aim to reduce expenditure on Housing Benefit, it has been successful in reducing the expectations of low-income social housing tenants. Alongside other welfare changes it embeds the idea that the welfare state will be further eroded. It appears, to these tenants at least, that welfare reform marks the beginning of the end of the welfare state as they knew it – a welfare state which would protect them from the 'cradle to the grave'.

When UC is implemented tenants will receive their Housing Benefit paid directly to them, making them responsible for paying their rent to the housing association rather than it being deducted at source. Ruby worried about how she would manage this forthcoming change: "it always plays on my mind. Once they start this, where they give you the money to pay the whole rent, I'll dip into it, especially if I'm struggling or summat and he needs summat." She is concerned about how she will adapt and prioritise rent payments when her child is in need materially. However, adapt she must, because if she fails to adhere to the neoliberal mantra of individual responsibility she may find herself in the same position as Marlene and those others whose failure to deal with, and adapt to, the benefit changes has resulted in homelessness and displacement. Ruby is already in rent arrears and has had her application for DHP rejected because she has not rejoined the social housing register and is seen as not actively looking to downsize. What her housing status will be in the future depends on the choices she now makes; she can choose to cut back further and try to remain in her home, or she must take active steps to clear her arrears and downsize. Alternatively, Ruby could look for work in the now normalised flexible, low-waged labour market, and work to overcome the barriers she has to employment: age, lack of skills and mental health issues. These are ultimately the options she is faced with as the 'status of being *on* welfare is replaced by the transitory experience of being processed (back) into work *through* workfare' (Peck 2001: 12) in order 'to "churn" the welfare/workfare population, to hold them close to or push them into the job market, and to systematically remove alternative means of support in order to enforce (low) wage dependency' (Peck 2001: 12). For these tenants, it feels as though they are living through the demise of the welfare state, what Wacquant (2013: 8) would call the 'reengineering of the state'. This is the sociology of neoliberalism, the 'building of a particular kind of state' (Wacquant 2013: 1) to which people have to become accustomed and adaptable to if they want to remain in their homes.

Housing precarity and advanced marginality in the UK

This book began with a historical overview of the origins and development of council housing in the UK. While the foundations of the present-day social housing system were laid down in the years following the First World War, calls for state intervention in the housing market had their roots in the latter years of the 19th century. Chapter 2 started from the need to acquire a historical understanding of housing inequality by looking at a time when council/social housing or a fully functioning welfare state did not exist. This is important, as it appears that both are in the process of being eroded. In the years preceding the rise of council housing the private sector dominated but was unable to meet the housing demands of a growing population. The private sector is once again growing in prominence as social housing at a social rent is declining in favour of 'affordable' rents, starter homes and help-to-buy schemes. The loss of social housing and the undermining of council estates will increase housing precarity for those on the lowest incomes, and is likely to increase homelessness and return those on the lowest incomes to the pre-council estate era of squalid and cramped, privately rented accommodation. Moreover, this will lead to advanced marginality and rising discontent and anger. As Chapter 2 made clear, housing issues are a major source of tension precisely because housing is resource that we all need.

In the wake of the Great Recession of 2008–9, the worst in British history since the Great Depression of the 1930s, the Conservative-led Coalition government used the crisis conditions to implement far-reaching austerity measures that have impacted on large swaths of the population in ways that are still not fully understood. Austerity was used to launch a full-scale attack on the UK's social security system. Cuts to Housing Benefit inflicted deeper poverty and have greatly increased housing precarity. Housing is a political issue and has long been used as a political tool to undermine opposition parties and to garner votes. In the context of the UK, the policies implemented by the former Coalition government and the following Conservative government elected to power in 2015 have resulted in division. Just as the housing question in Victorian Britain led to rising resentment and anger, so too are the policies inflicted by the government today leading to greater resentment at the local level and political dissatisfaction more broadly. History is always important. Chapter 2 highlighted the local and political tensions that flared up around the housing question and how, with concerted political will, the state sought to relieve the distress that housing need engendered. The implementation of the welfare state following Beveridge's famous report led to the rise of the council estate and a welfare system that would protect people from the worst excesses of the capitalist system and, in terms of housing, would reduce the 'squalor' that Beveridge saw as the condition of housing in 1942.

However, it was only with the introduction of locally administered rent rebate schemes in the 1970s that provision was made for assistance to council tenants in low-paid work, or those otherwise ineligible for help from the national assistance scheme. The introduction of the Housing Benefit scheme in 1982 increased housing security for low-income earners. The scheme was designed to address three main issues: to shift subsidies away from 'bricks and mortar' and towards means-tested personal subsidies; to improve housing affordability; and to act as a safety net to prevent post-rent incomes from falling below a certain level (Stephens 2005). Despite the difficulties in implementing these reforms, they were important in the context of rising unemployment in the 1970s and 1980s as deindustrialisation wrought havoc in many working-class communities and of social changes that saw the decline of nuclear-family structures and a rise in female part-time employment.

However, the ensuing rise of neoliberalism as a political–economic project saw the privatisation of council housing, alongside the rising stigmatisation of council estates. Over the intervening years this stigmatisation has blossomed and grown so that council housing began to be seen as an agent of 'social exclusion' and so-called 'benefit dependency'. The rise of Thatcherism in the 1980s sowed the seeds of the housing crisis that we find ourselves in today. The RTB policy has left a lasting legacy, as the homes sold were not replaced. Nevertheless, inequalities in labour incomes and an increasing skill divide were mitigated by a responsive welfare state. The New Labour welfare project was concerned with changing the behaviours of welfare recipients in order to engage them in waged work in the context of a changing labour market. While the conditionality of benefits was tightened, New Labour also introduced the National Minimum Wage and expanded in-work benefits in the form of Working Tax Credits and childcare support in order to make work pay. In the sphere of housing, however, their policies were seen as a continuation of what had gone before.

Nevertheless, their redistribution policies resulted in a steady income growth for those on the lowest incomes; but from 2011 onwards this came to an abrupt halt (Fetzer 2018). The reversal reached its zenith in the onslaught that followed the financial crash and the implementation of austerity measures. Moreover, the huge raft of welfare changes was legitimated by the narrative of 'fairness' which pitted 'ordinary' working people against other groups that became drawn into the new 'undeserving'. In the years since, food bank use and homelessness have risen, alongside increasing child poverty. While this book presents one case study of one social policy there is a wider issue here about the way in which cuts to Housing Benefit are impacting on people and communities. Commentators and charities have all expressed concern that further cuts, which at the time of writing are now being rolled out, will result in rising rent arrears and evictions.

Despite the fact that council/social housing and the estates in which it is located have been the subject of critique, and bound up with notions of 'benefit dependency', people were born, lived and died in council housing. It housed generations of families and still does, despite the fact that many on a low income are increasingly being pushed out or denied access to the sector. Historically, housing has been a source of tension and unrest, as was evidenced by the report into industrial unrest that was commissioned by David Lloyd George in 1917. He was the person credited with pioneering the welfare state. However, the housing security that was enabled by nearly 60 years of rent support is being eroded and the availability of truly 'affordable' social housing is declining, leading to higher rates of people housed in temporary accommodation – often in hotels, bed and breakfast establishments and homeless hostels – and rising street homelessness. The moral indignation that is levelled at those on low incomes has not changed either. Those experiencing poverty are lambasted for their low-income status and blamed for their poverty. The Commissioners' report into industrial unrest in 1917 found housing to be a major cause of frustration as the eviction rate grew and people had to do moonlight flits because of rent arrears. To be sure, we are living in very different times but tensions around housing access and affordability are growing among those at the sharp end of the housing affordability crisis, aided and abetted by the retraction of rent support. As this book has demonstrated in Chapters 3 and 4, people are increasingly doing moonlight flits and abandoning properties to escape rent arrears and formal eviction. And it appears that we are returning to the days when both the private sector and the social sector become unaffordable to those most in need as landlords become risk averse to the new model of Housing Benefit support. The accumulation of arrears inflicts a crushing blow on mind and body as people reduce their expenditure on food and fuel to meet the rent, and experience the psychological distress of potentially losing both a home *and* community.

To explore the impact, effect or influence of the Bedroom Tax, it is necessary to establish what went before and what came after in order to define what the impacts (material, social, financial or psychological) are. The participants in this study correspond to the wider demographic population of social housing tenants. They were all on low incomes because of sickness, economic inactivity or under-employment and, as such, claimed Housing Benefit to cover the cost of or to top up their rent. As was shown in Chapter 2, the development of the Housing Benefit scheme was a vitally important mechanism enabling those in the most precarious situations to be housed. The participants in this study were in a precarious economic position prior to the introduction of the Bedroom Tax policy and when it came into force on 1 April 2013 they had to find around an extra £60–100 per month for rent. The impact was a cut in the household budget, primarily for expenditure on food (see Chapter 4). Cuts in expenditure were made in an effort to remain living in the property, because in the first few months of its introduction the majority (27 of 31) of participants had made no attempt to downsize. These participants absorbed the extra rental outgoings by reducing expenditure on food and fuel and curtailing expenditure on less pressing bills, socialising and non-essential children's items and treats. The impacts were material, resulting in food and fuel poverty and accentuating austerity measures at the household level.

However, a more significant outcome, arguably, was the impact which the policy had on psychological health. The policy did not just take away a portion of a tenant's income; it introduced a feeling of housing insecurity which had not been there previously, and this insecurity was transmitted to other members of the household. This had psychological impacts, what Bragg et al (2015: 82) liken to a feeling of 'psychological homelessness'. It was the ongoing pressure to pay the Bedroom Tax, the emotional labour involved in maintaining a facade of normalcy when rent arrears accrued, that began to affect participants psychologically as they began to fear that they might lose their tenancies. Depression, anxiety, anger, apathy and tearfulness were manifest; they suffered the 'pathologies of precarity' (Davies nd), which are injurious to physical and emotional wellbeing. Precarity of income and work paled in significance when compared to the feeling engendered by housing precarity. This raises the question of why it was that participants did not seek to stabilise their housing situations by swapping homes or downsizing. Put simply, participants wanted to remain in their homes; they had invested in them financially and emotionally and it was only at the point of crisis, when catching up with arrears seemed untenable, or when they received threats of repossession, that this action was prompted.

Paradoxically, it was at this point, outlined in Chapter 4, that the relationship between agency and structure brought into sharp focus the lack of foresight inherent in the policy-making process. Housing associations had their own discretionary rules about allowing mobility within their own housing sector. Before tenants could move, the largest social housing provider in Tarley required them to bring their property up to a standard of condition that the housing association deemed appropriate but which cost tenants money, adding further financial pressure. Further, the housing association did not allow tenants with rent arrears to move. The financial constraints that participants were under, and their poor skills in accessing and then navigating the internet to search for a new home, were exacerbated by the dearth of smaller properties. Trying to remain in their homes was a form of resistance, but the pressures of doing so ground people down emotionally. The home, as a source of stability, became a burden, but release from that burden placed tenants up against a new set of constraints, which for some left them with no apparent way out of the situation. This led to a pathway of housing precarity, which is understood here as the *process* through which housing insecurity was engendered. Analytically, this constitutes a housing-centred approach to precarity rather than one linked to labour market relations. This approach is adopted because, although, biographically, employment instability was the norm (Shildrick et al 2012) – and, indeed, is a defining feature of contemporary working-class life – Housing Benefit had acted as a buffer to housing insecurity, providing stability in the face of labour market uncertainty. The Bedroom Tax, however, induced housing precarity by reducing Housing Benefit at source. The participants in this study all had their Housing Benefit paid directly to their social landlord. If the same amount of money had been cut from income they actually received in their hand they would have still struggled financially, but their housing costs would have been covered and their housing security would have remained intact.

Wacquant's (2008) attention to the relationship between the advancement of urban marginality and the retrenchment of Western welfare states is useful for understanding the way welfare state policies can be instruments to coerce, control or change a cultural perception about what the state will provide to whom and why. In the UK context, social housing was born of a government commitment to eradicate slums and provide housing after the destruction wrought by the Second World War. The so-called 'wobbly pillar under the welfare state' (Torgersen 1987), it was a project mired in controversy. State-provided, stable, good-quality, affordable housing for the working classes became, it appeared, representative of 'Britain's social sickness' (Hanley 2012: xiii). In recent years, social housing has been much maligned. However, the action of undermining the stability that social housing affords low-income populations does not incentivise work. Many people who claim rent support *do* work. Being evicted from social housing or losing a tenancy through the accumulation of arrears contributes to urban marginality, as those people find themselves homeless and insecurely housed. Their losses are multiple: home, shelter, social networks and their sense of belonging. Under these circumstances people become more concerned with trying to secure a place to live as opposed to looking for work.

In the UK context, there is a link between the retrenchment of the welfare state and the role Housing Benefit plays in mitigating the forces of advanced marginality. It is the vital link between being securely housed and becoming insecurely housed or homeless. As a means to induce behavioural change to move or find work, in order to address the supposed 'culture of worklessness and dependency' (DWP 2010a: 2), the policy failed to consider the meanings that tenants attached to their homes. Social housing provided people with ontological security *and* ontological anchorage. The depictions of social housing by think-tanks, journalists and politicians as 'nightmarish' and 'obsolete' (Slater 2013: 384) are in contrast to how tenants themselves view it: they know its worth. When homeownership cannot be a consideration and the PRS is deemed costly and insecure, social housing is a resource that is hugely valued.

Chapters 5 and 6 demonstrated empirically that policy prescriptions are sometimes completely divorced from real-world processes. As argued by Gibb (2015: 155), 'policies such as the Bedroom Tax were opportunistic ideas with no evidentiary basis whatsoever'. Tenants did not behave in a way that the policy sought to make them behave; those with ill-health were in no fit state to consider employment, while those who were employed struggled to find employment that would pay enough to release them from claiming Housing Benefit. The struggle to keep the home became untenable as rent arrears accrued, particularly for those who had pre-existing arrears. To avoid the threat of eviction some tenants found social housing in a different borough, while others moved into the PRS, which cost more in Housing

Benefit. Abandoning a property before formal eviction takes place avoids a humiliating public spectacle; it is a response to the indignity of not managing to cope – and there is no dignity in fighting eviction, which is often a public process that shows the world your inability to manage. Lorey (2015) contends that it is through precarity that the state governs; it reinforces responsibilisation and shifts the duty of social security from the state onto the individual. A Foucauldian analysis of how shame and poverty can become a 'technology of the self', shaping behaviour to avoid showing publicly an inability to cope, is instructive in illustrating the way the re-engineering of the state is enabled (Wacquant 2012). Subjects do have agency, and the state, via the Bedroom Tax policy, places individuals in a situation whereby they must choose the appropriate course of action to take. Irrespective of the structural and financial constraints, they have to live with the consequence of their actions. Ultimately, they assist in the re-engineering of the neoliberal state as they learn to accept the neoliberal logic of welfare state 'devolution, retraction and recomposition' outlined by Wacquant (2012: 72). The Bedroom Tax illustrates how protective forms of welfare become 'corrective welfare' which 'entails specific behavioural mandates' (Wacquant 2012: 72). However, accepting the neoliberal logic of welfare state retrenchment entails more than the practicalities of behavioural change. It also needs to invoke a symbolic shift in perception.

As was discussed in Chapter 5, one of the impacts of the Bedroom Tax was that it shifted participants' perceptions about the role of social housing. There was an evident culture of entitlement; people viewed social housing properties as homes that were theirs – not in the sense of homeownership, but in the sense that they would be able to occupy homes indefinitely. This was a right afforded in the Housing Act 1980. There was also an absence of fear that they would be required to vacate their homes arbitrarily, which is a common occurrence in the PRS. To a certain extent the Bedroom Tax shifted these perceptions; it conveyed unequivocally that illness, disability or having dependent children would not shield you from having to forgo your property if it was deemed unsuitable for your needs. Housing associations do not need to implement fixed term tenure in order to make housing insecure – the government can do so by reducing the financial means that enables tenants to remain in their properties. Housing Benefit is a central component in maintaining housing stability because it is this, rather than tenure rights, that enables those on low incomes to be housed. As Cowen and Marsh (forthcoming) make clear, the Bedroom Tax has become 'a symbol of austerity measures seen by many as draconian and punitive'. However, despite the widespread condemnation of the policy by opposition parties, charities and the UN Special Rapporteur on housing on account of the hardship it is causing, there has been no shift on the part of government to abolish it. Arguably, because its significance is ideological it is about remaking the role of social housing, and a remaking of the state and of welfare more broadly. From providing long-term security, social housing is being reconfigured to meet 'temporary and transient housing need' (Cowen and Marsh forthcoming) in what will be left of the homes that are available at a social rent. This fundamentally changes the culture of social housing, and it will potentially change the culture of those communities dependent on it. On estates such as Tarley it was, centrally, the longevity of residents, coupled with institutions such as the social club, which brought people together and gave them a sense of community. Generational bonds of family and friends were forged precisely because people were immobile. Historically, temporary or transient housing provision would not have facilitated that. Moreover, there is a flip side to undermining symbolically and practically the long-term stability that social housing has afforded tenants.

Chapter 6 outlined how tenants viewed the Bedroom Tax, addressing the question of what participants thought about the policy and why they felt it had been implemented. By focusing on their voices, it became clear that their thoughts and opinions inextricably tied together issues of immigration and housing shortage. The threat of losing housing stability provoked a nativist response, expressed in the opinion that it was the need to house the greater number of newcomers moving into the area that was the core reason for the policy. This undermines solidarity and community cohesion because it ratchets up the sense of competition, the feeling there is not enough to go around. Therefore, being British born and bred serves as a marker of legitimating claims to resources because, for some, it is the only claim to entitlement they can make. The discourses of devaluation, and the way that the policy targeted only those who claimed Housing Benefit support, reinforced the idea among participants that they were at the losing end for physical and symbolic resources. The devaluation of the culture and class of benefit-claiming social housing tenants, both depicted as deficit in the opinion of participants, is viewed as a way to legitimate the undermining of home, social ties and community. Participants did not own anything in the way of savings or property except for the possessions they had accumulated. Housing stability, localised social ties and the feeling that they had some sort of community of provenance were the only assets – intangible as they were

— that they did possess. These were important for psychological and practical reasons. To appreciate what participants felt they were losing is to understand what they felt they had before the implementation of the policy. It represented more than potentially losing a home. Since there were no guarantees that they could be rehoused within the neighbourhood, it threatened their whole way of life, their place in the world, the place where they had put down roots, knew people and were known. To destabilise that, to induce ontological insecurity and threaten ontological anchorage, is to cultivate feelings of fear and resentment: fear that your place in the world is of little value, that others will supplant you, fear of what the future holds, because if your home can be taken, what else will be taken and what future is there for your children? There is a psychological importance to place that transcends bricks, mortar, streets and neighbourhood institutions; community can be representative of the sum of the parts of social bonds enabled by housing stability and longevity. Moreover, as this study suggests, these social bonds are important assets in helping to mitigate the hardships of poverty, particularly for lone parents and those with health issues; they are the prop in an informal system of welfare support at the local level, which is hugely significant when those provided by the state are being curtailed. One might conclude that the 'Big Society' is already in place and in operation at the local level and that government policies such as the Bedroom Tax will work to undermine it rather than foster it.

There is no pride to be had in being labelled as 'welfare dependent'; dependency denotes a devalued status — "the lowest of the low", as one participant put it. However, participants were up against the structural constraints of the job market and the personal constraints of caring responsibilities and ill-health. The sense of powerlessness and the feeling of being bullied and forced to downsize ran deep, building on pre-existing resentments and creating new ones. For the study participants, the policy was one of involuntary removal that created a sense of injustice and anger. Other research on the Bedroom Tax has drawn attention to how the policy increases resentment and undermines community cohesion. This book has gone one step further: through a greater focus and analysis on the meanings attached to the policy, as detailed in Chapters 5 and 6, it concludes that the Bedroom Tax is, inherently, a divisive social policy. It causes people to judge and point the finger at others in the same social position. In this sense it constitutes an inward-looking replay of the deserving and undeserving characterisations propagated by politicians and the media, built upon discourses that 'other' and 'blame' (Peacock et al 2014: 178).

This divisiveness over low-cost housing represents a conflict within classes rather than between them.

The Bedroom Tax has wider social impacts that go beyond inducing a greater level of material poverty. At the neighbourhood level it is perceived by participants as an attack on culture. To introduce into people's lives a policy that displaces and replaces people because of worklessness and economic insecurity, and without an adequate amount of smaller homes to manage it, is nothing short of a "conscious cruelty" (Loach 2016: 00.00.01/00.00.31). This policy shows a blatant disregard for the interconnectedness of people's lives and the importance of home and locality in shaping people's sense of belonging and security. The backlash to that is greater resentment, played out at the local level and articulated through hierarchies of belonging (Skey 2014). When so much is working against people's ability to remain in their homes and communities, when people feel socially rejected, devalued and forcibly removed, nativism will manifest and communalist bonds and claims to entitlement will be staked (Amin 2002; Yuval-Davis et al 2005; Wrenn 2014). In contrast to Wacquant's assertion that territorial stigmatisation leads people to disassociate with 'neighbourhoods of relegation', this study has shown that place came to matter *more*. As stigmatised as people felt their community was, they saw it as theirs; when they felt that their place in the neighbourhood could be supplanted by 'others' whom they viewed as less entitled than them, place attachment was reinforced. As one participant described, "it might be a shithole, but it's our home big time".

The rise of housing precarity

Since the implementation of austerity measures, homelessness in England in each of its various forms has risen, with a report by the National Audit Office (NAO 2017) highlighting the 60% increase in households in temporary accommodation since 2011. Alongside this there has been a 63% rise in households threatened with homelessness and helped to remain in their home by local authorities, as well as a staggering 134% increase in rough sleepers since 2010 (Fitzpatrick et al 2017). Further, since 2011 the UK has witnessed a 248% increase in households placed in temporary accommodation outside the local authority that recorded them as homeless (NAO 2017). This research has demonstrated that the Bedroom Tax has contributed to eviction and housing abandonment, but this is just one policy among many. Following on the heels of the changes to Housing Benefit laid out in the Welfare Reform Act 2012, in 2015 the newly elected Conservative government announced further Housing Benefit changes as part of the July 2015 budget. These comprised freezes to LHA rates for four years from 2016, the removal of Housing Benefit from people aged 18 to 21 (with some exceptions) and a further reduction in the household Benefit Cap. While housing benefit for those under 21 has been reinstated amid fears of rising youth homelessness, significantly the household Benefit Cap results in reduced Housing Benefit entitlement for those above the cap threshold, so it is, essentially, a cut in Housing Benefit. Research has shown that the freezing of LHA rates alone will mean that by 2019–20 four-fifths (83%) of housing in England will be unaffordable to LHA claimants (Shelter 2017). These are deeply worrying trends and, if the impact of the Bedroom Tax is anything to go by, they will have extremely adverse impacts.

While the government has sought to mitigate the effects of the cuts via the use of DHP at the local level, councils use their 'discretion' to allocate funds. DHP may be refused on various grounds – for example, if a tenant is not seen to be actively looking to downsize. Moreover, the fund is a short-term measure which will not meet a long-term need. The reduction in Housing Benefit has had an effect on the way in which both the social sector and the PRS allocate housing. Social landlords are increasingly conducting 'affordability checks', and if a prospective tenant cannot demonstrate that they can afford the rent, then the allocation may be seen as unviable and the application may be declined (Barnes 2017). Fitzpatrick et al's (2017) online survey of local authorities reported problems for homeless applicants in accessing social tenancies. Moreover, it was noted that housing associations 'are becoming increasingly selective regarding applicant incomes and independent living skills' (Fitzpatrick et al 2017: x). Fitzpatrick et al suggest that:

> The capacity of the social rented sector to meet housing needs will continue to be tested in the years ahead, despite the new Government's injection of funds to modestly increase the supply of affordable housing from 2017/18. (Fitzpatrick et al 2017: x)

Accessing the PRS is also becoming increasingly difficult for those who rely on rent support. Half of local authorities in England, and almost all in London, reported difficulties in assisting their homeless applicants into the sector. Data obtained from local authorities revealed that people's ability to pay rising rents was being eroded by welfare reforms (Fitzpatrick et al 2017).

Despite the fact that academics, housing groups, charities and commentators have highlighted and raised concern about the impact of welfare reforms, the government have failed to fully assess the impact of the reforms on homelessness. As a result, we do not know how many households would have been homeless if the reforms had not been implemented (Fitzpatrick et al 2017; NAO 2017). Moreover, research examining the cumulative impacts of welfare reforms (EHRC 2018) has highlighted the disproportionate impact of cuts on protected groups. The EHRC (2018: 24) report urged the government, 'as a matter of urgency', to review the level of benefits to ensure that they provide an adequate standard of living. Other legislation, such as the Housing and Planning Act 2016, may negatively impact on homelessness, amid concerns that voluntary RTB for housing associations and the mandatory sale of high-value council housing will further deplete the stock of available housing (Fitzpatrick et al 2017). The current roll-out of UC is set to make things harder still, causing the PRS to 'introduce blanket policies against claimants' (Shelter 2017: 4). What's more, private landlords are also restricted in letting to Housing Benefit claimants, as mortgage and insurance rules ban many landlords from renting to this demographic in what can only be described as blatant discrimination. Private landlords are well aware that their role in housing future generations will increase as the ability of social housing to provide a 'home for life' and access to the sector decrease. Many small landlords own and let out property as asset-based welfare, and are reluctant to house those experiencing poverty and increasing urban marginality. Their properties are an asset that will contribute towards their pension or retirement; they will afford them healthcare or can be passed on as inheritance. They do not want or need the economic uncertainty of housing those who potentially will fall into rent arrears.

Housing association officers, working at the front-line of these changes, are having to deal with a situation they have little control over when rent arrears are accrued. Many of the participants in this study found their local housing officer to be helpful when it came to helping them downsize. This was the case with Jimmy, whose worsening illness due to cancer made it difficult for him to use the stairs in his block of flats. He was helped to move to a smaller property more suited to his needs, albeit it in a different neighbourhood. Others, however, felt patronised and felt that they received little empathy when arrears mounted up. The housing officer I spoke with did not support the use of Fixed Term Tenancies, as he felt they would deter tenants from investing in their houses as homes. Further, he suggested that if the government really wanted to ensure the long-term viability of social housing, then they should not be selling it off at huge discounts. For him, this would only lead to profit making and the likelihood that these homes would end up in the PRS. In the coming years housing associations will face a tension between their mission to support vulnerable households and the increasing business incentive to move towards housing those who have the means to pay their own rents.

Divisive social policy

In the political debates about the consequences of austerity policies, the suggestion that austerity has divisive social effects is conspicuous by its absence. However, since the vote to leave the European Union in 2016 notions about a divided Britain have gained in prominence. Winlow et al (2017) argue that anyone who has had close experience of the lives of the post-industrial working class cannot have failed to notice their hardening attitudes and deteriorating conditions. For some sections of the working class these conditions are set to get worse, not better, as the changes outlined in this book continue to impact on those with the fewest housing options and as solidarity between groups is undermined by damaging rhetoric that pits people against each other in the struggle for resources and social respect.

While new initiatives to deal with rising homelessness are being piloted, until the government faces up to the fact that it is their welfare reforms that are helping to drive the increase in housing precarity and homelessness, these initiatives will attempt to fix the symptoms and not the cause. The problem is not going away. This issue should not be a matter of party politics; it needs a remedy that is rooted in consensus, so that those most in need do not become priced out of the housing market completely. Housing is a political issue, and history reminds us that it leads to tensions which have political repercussions. Housing was a central part of Lloyd George's social reform policies in 1919. Fraser sums up the situation in 1919 that drove forward political action on housing:

> A vigorous housing programme offered tangible gains to the working class from the existing political structure ... Housing policies thus became part of the insurance against revolution where the undoubted public cost could be written off as a necessary premium on social stability. As Lloyd George reminded the cabinet in 1919, 'Even if it cost

a hundred million pounds, what was that compared to the stability of the state?' (Fraser 1973/1984: 181)

In 1919 there was political fear about the spread of 'Bolshevism'. In today's Britain the current political fears, arguably, relate to rising nationalism. English Nationalism in particular has been on the rise in recent years. In her ethnographic study of the English Defence League, Pilkington (2016: 159) drew attention to the anger that housing issues create, noting how 'housing [was] the most contentious issue' when respondents spoke about perceived competition over housing resources. The Bedroom Tax has made this situation worse because it is viewed as forced displacement and abandonment. Nowicki (2014: 127) extends Porteous and Smith's (2001) concept of 'domicide', defined as the intentional destruction or displacement from the material home, to understand 'the ways in which home can be deliberately destroyed socially and symbolically'. She asserts that in the 'current global sociopolitical landscape, domicide and its impact is writ large'. Similarly, Paton and Cooper (2016) argue that the state is implicit in domicide through its enactment of policies that restrict rent support, thus rendering rents unaffordable in what amounts to 'state led eviction'. Indeed, as this book has demonstrated, this is in line with what many of the tenants in this study felt when they talked about being pushed, bullied and forced from their homes. Under these circumstances, and alongside other welfare cuts and collapsing social services, it is not surprising that anger would ensue. It has created local resentment and tension and, some argue, austerity policies have resulted in a political backlash. Research by Fetzer (2018) analysing what caused the vote to leave the European Union in 2016 asserts that austerity policies played a major part. He suggests that from around 2005 incomes fell for those at the lower end of the skill divide, while they rose for those at the end of the human capital divide. The redistribution policies of New Labour's Brown administration (2007–10) mitigated the effect of this growing inequality, but were derailed by the financial crisis. Using quantitative analysis of voting behaviour, Fetzer (2018: 3) cites the Bedroom Tax as one of the policies which 'caused the upheavals in the UK's political landscape'. He focused on three reforms in particular: the abolition of centrally funded Council Tax Benefit, the reform of DLA and the Bedroom Tax. What must be noted here is that many people were affected cumulatively by these cuts, as this book has highlighted. Fetzer argues that those who were exposed to these reforms were more likely to have generated grievances that had a bearing on political preferences, his central argument being that austerity 'was key to *activating these grievances*, converting them into political dissatisfaction culminating in Brexit' (Fetzer 2018: 5).

Arguably, the grievances of the post-industrial working class have been brewing for decades as poverty and inequality have grown since the late 1970s, in tandem with the rise of neoliberalism, the loss of industries, the rise of the service sector economy, automation and the normalisation of precarious employment. This has also impacted on labour-based solidarities, which have coalesced with the intensification of damaging representations of the working class and feelings of being increasingly politically voiceless. Becker and Fetzer (2018) suggest that austerity has undermined the capacity of the welfare state to mitigate the effects of these longer-running economic trends, which may have affected support for trade integration or migration. For these authors it appears that:

> immigration was not supported by accommodating fiscal policies, such as support for housing construction and general improvements in the ability of public services to cope with increased demand for services … Remember that in the wake of the financial crisis, the British government set out on a period of fiscal austerity with dramatic effects on public spending. Increased demand for public services was met with austerity. While this did not erode the relative rates of access to the welfare state by UK-born residents living in areas more affected by migration from Eastern Europe, competition over increasingly difficult-to-access services might have been (rightly or wrongly) interpreted as being associated with immigration. (Becker and Fetzer 2018)

This book supports this prognosis, as it is towards immigration that resentment around housing is directed. Winlow et al (2017: 2) attribute rising nationalism to the failure of the political establishment to address the concerns of the post-industrial working class, whose fears are dismissed 'as irrational and counterproductive to the continual flourishing of progressive cultural life'. Many of the participants in this study felt that politicians were completely out of touch with the realities of their lives, expressed in statements such as "do they know what they are doing to people?" and "they should come and live like we do". Taylor-Gooby (2016: 715) argues that the financial crisis provided the Conservative Party with the opportunity to permanently shrink the welfare state. He suggests that in the past the welfare state played a key role in achieving a measure of social cohesion; however, this becomes harder to maintain as political trust declines and governments have less to offer a more fragmented electorate. As such, he suggests that 'one strategy is to use social policy in a divisive way to advantage key groups of supporters and to denigrate and stigmatize non-supporters. UK governments since 2010 have been particularly active in doing this' (Taylor-Gooby 2016: 717). What is concerning is that many of the changes to the social security system that were initiated under the banner of austerity are still in the messy process of being implemented. UC is one such policy. As for the Bedroom Tax, while the devolved governments of Scotland and Northern Ireland have largely protected their social housing tenants from its effects, how long they can continue to do so remains open to question. Northern Ireland in particular presents a worrying case, given that their mitigation package is in place only until 2020. If this money is withdrawn, it would mean that up to 30,000[1] people in the province could become liable to pay. In Belfast there is a history of conflict around housing and many communities are still segregated along political and religious lines.

As this research has demonstrated, the Bedroom Tax is a policy that causes resentment and division within and between the working-class. As the housing options of those at the lower end of the class structure are set to become more restricted in the coming years we will see the rise of advanced marginality and its associated repercussions, and the continuing divide between the haves and the have-nots.

The making of advanced marginality

The retrenchment of the welfare state that has taken place in the UK since 2010 and the deepening housing precarity that has ensued are the mechanism which will create more advanced marginalisation. As this book has demonstrated, the deteriorating social and economic conditions that austerity has inflicted have been met with anger and rage. As well as a declining welfare state, the functioning of the informal welfare state that operates at the local level through kin and friendship networks is being eroded as working-class solidarity and community longevity are undermined. This book has aimed not only to show the impacts of the Bedroom Tax but to make clear more broadly the centrality of housing to social and political stability. Who will get to speak on behalf of, and seek to represent, those who feel critically disengaged from the mainstream? We are living in turbulent political times. Wacquant (1999: 1641) argues that the tell-tale signs of urban marginality can be seen in rising homelessness, teeming soup kitchens, the rising despondency and rage of the unemployed and under-employed, as well as increasing xenophobia, racial violence and 'hostility towards and amongst the poor'. This is indeed what we are seeing in the UK, although, for some, this aspect of austerity seems to have passed them by. In 2018 *The Guardian* newspaper asked the UK's homelessness minister why rough sleeping had been increasing year on year for seven years. She responded, 'in truth, I don't know'.[2] The Bedroom Tax is an insidious policy that proceeds to wear down the most vulnerable in subtle and gradual ways, as this research has shown, it can and does lead some of the most vulnerable down a path that may end in homelessness. Add to this the cuts to LHA rates and the SAR, and it is no wonder that we are seeing the signs of urban marginality in rising food bank use and visibly rising levels of rough sleeping.

One of the central arguments in this book has been that Wacquant's (2008) analysis of the causes and signs of advanced urban marginality does reflect, to a great extent, the changing nature of rent support and social housing in the UK; the former, in its role of preventing urban marginality, through recourse to obtaining and sustaining housing and preventing homelessness; the latter in its changing of tenant composition in favour of those with the means to afford rents. Increases in house builds of varying tenures may go some way to addressing the UK's housing crisis, but if the means through which people are able to access and sustain that housing are undermined by continuing cuts to Housing Benefit, then we will see greater housing precarity and the attendant march of advanced marginality. Mark Blyth's (2013) assertion that austerity is a dangerous idea would appear to be correct. A political vacuum is opening up in the UK, just as it was the case when the Labour Party first rose to power on the back of widespread discontent. Housing was a major factor then, and we forget the centrality of housing to political stability at our peril. Left unchecked, this housing precarity may take us back decades, and once again make housing insecurity the norm for vast swaths of the UK population, returning working-class families to an era of squalid, privately rented accommodation such that the building of public housing sought to help eradicate. The Bedroom Tax, and other policies like it that result in cuts to Housing Benefit, will not deal with the housing affordability crisis in the UK. On the contrary, these policies will work only to intensify it. Widening income inequalities and powerful financial and corporate interests are proceeding apace. Those who seek political office will need to offer the electorate an alternative vision of a more equitable future, a future that is not built upon the lie that gains from economic growth will benefit all. Moreover, they will need to offer a politics of hope rather than a politics of regression.

Appendix

Respondent set chart

Pseudonym	Gender	Age	Ethnicity (self-declared)	Employment status	Accommodation type
Betty	Female	51	White British	Not employed (ESA)	3 bedroom house
Marina	Female	41	White British	Not employed (ESA)	3 bedroom house
Jessica	Female	56	White British	Not employed (ESA)	3 bedroom house
Mary	Female	59	British/Mixed Race	Unemployed (JSA)	3 bedroom house
Mo	Female	57	White British	Not employed (Carer)	3 bedroom house
Mick	Male	56	White British	Not employed (DLA)	3 bedroom house
Rory	Male	55	White British	Not employed (DLA)	2 bedroom flat
Louise	Female	38	British/Mixed Race	In part-time employment	4 bedroom house
Tracey	Female	56	White British	Not employed (Carer)	3 bedroom house
Billy	Male	52	White British	Not employed (Carer)	3 bedroom house
Sheila	Female	51	White British	Not employed (DLA)	3 bedroom house
Jimmy	Male	55	White British	Not employed (DLA)	2 bedroom flat
Annie	Female	49	White British	Not employed (DLA)	2 bedroom house
Cath	Female	28	White British	Unemployed	4 bedroom house
Fiona	Female	50	White British	In part-time employment	5 bedroom house
Eric	Male	40	White British	Unemployed (JSA)	3 bedroom house
Mark	Male	50	White British	Unemployed (JSA)	3 bedroom house

Family status	Length of residence in home	Length of residence within Tarley	Housing outcomes
Lives with one child	17 years	17 years	Downsized within Tarley (social housing)
Lived with one child	20 years	41 years	Deceased
Living alone	9 years	56 years	Downsized within Tarley (social housing)
Living alone	30 years	41 years	Downsized within Tarley (social housing)
Lives with (cares for) adult son	33 years	33 years	Remains in home
Living alone	11 years	56 years	Downsized out of Tarley (social housing)
Living alone	15 years	55 years	Remains in home
Lives with 3 daughters	8 years	32 years	Remains in home
Lives with (cares for) husband	30 years	56 years	Remains in home
Living with (cares for disabled) wife	20 years	40 years	Downsized within Tarley (social housing)
Living with husband (he is her carer)	23 years	32 years	Remains in home
Living alone	14 years	39 years	Downsized out of Tarley (social housing)
Living alone	30 years	31 years	Remains in home
Living with four children (3 girls, 1 boy)	9 years	28 years	Accrued arrears through Bedroom Tax. Evicted after the Benefit Cap was implemented. Currently in temporary accommodation
Living with husband, 1 daughter and 2 grandchildren	15 years	50 years	Downsized out of Tarley (PRS)
Living with two children (1 girl, 1 boy)	9 years	39 years	Evicted (abandoned property before formal eviction). Lives in social housing outside the city boundary
Living with daughter	15 years	15 years	Remains in home

(continued)

Respondent set chart (continued)

Pseudonym	Gender	Age	Ethnicity (self-declared)	Employment status	Accommodation type
June	Female	51	White British	Not in Employment (DLA)	3 bedroom house
Teresa	Female	37	White British	Not in employment (ESA)	3 bedroom house
Patty	Female	54	White British	In part-time employment	2 bedroom maisonette
Don	Male	39	White British	Not in Employment (ESA)	2 bedroom flat
Ruby	Female	48	White British	Not in Employment (ESA)	3 bedroom house
Bob	Male	51	White British	Not in employment (Employment and Support Allowance)	3 bedroom house
Marlene	Female	50	White British	Not in employment (DLA)	3 bedroom house
Keith	Male	60	White British	Not in employment (ESA)	3 bedroom house
Emily	Female	51	White British	Not in employment (DLA)	2 bedroom house
Lisa	Female	42	White British	Not in employment (full-time mature student)	3 bedroom house
Jane	Female	45	White British	Under-employed (7 hours per week contract)	3 bedroom house
Katie	Female	48	White British	Not in employment (migrated from DLA to PIP)	3 bedroom house
Nadine	Female	44	White British	Not in Employment (DLA)	3 bedroom house
Shelly	Female	34	White British	Not in Employment (DLA)	2 bedroom flat

Family status	Length of residence in home	Length of residence within Tarley	Housing outcomes
Living alone	18 years	51 years	Downsized within Tarley (social housing)
Living with 2 daughters	10 years	30 years	Remains in home
Living with partner	29 years	29 years	Remains in home
Living alone. Daughter stays weekends and school holidays	3 years	39 years	Remains in home
Living with 1 son	19 years	40 years	Remains in home
Living alone	16 years	26 years	Remains in home – taken in a lodger
Living alone	15 years	40 years	Evicted (abandoned property before formal eviction), living in homeless hostel
Living alone	30 years	1 year	Downsized to Tarley via home exchange (social housing)
Living alone	3 years	10 years	Remains in home
Living with 2 sons	9 years	31 years	Remains in home
Living alone	17 years	28 years	Remains in home
Living with daughter	24 years	48 years	Downsized within Tarley (social housing)
Living alone	13 years	20 years	Downsized within Tarley via home exchange (social housing)
Living alone	1 year	25 years	Son has moved into property so no longer liable for Bedroom Tax

Notes

Chapter 1

[1] https://www.theguardian.com/society/2014/aug/12/stephanie-bottrill-worried-bedroom-tax-committed-suicide-coroner

Chapter 2

[1] www.branchcollective.org/?ps_articles=barbara-leckie-the-bitter-cry-of-outcast-london-1883-print-expose-and-print-reprise

[2] https://ia802706.us.archive.org/19/items/industrialunres00unregoog/industrialunres00unregoog.pdf

[3] https://www.centreforsocialjustice.org.uk/about/story

[4] www.politics.co.uk/comment-analysis/2010/10/4/george-osborne-speech-in-full

[5] 'No fines' is a concrete made without the sand. At the time, this process made for better insulation than traditional building materials, and allowed homes to be built quickly to meet increased demand for housing as workers flocked to the city during the boom years of the city's manufacturing base and other local industries.

[6] All participants are referred to by pseudonyms.

Chapter 5

[1] A Facebook status is a feature which allows users to discuss their thoughts with their friends on the Facebook social networking site.

[2] https://www.sundaypost.com/news/scottish-news/new-scheme-forces-experienced-tradesmen-back-to-school-or-out-of-a-job/

Chapter 7

[1] https://www.irishnews.com/news/2017/10/14/news/bedroom-tax-hits-northern-ireland-despite-political-pledges-1162165/

[2] https://www.theguardian.com/society/2018/mar/18/homelessness-minister-heather-wheeler-rough-sleeping-housing-first

References

Alber, J. (2010) 'What the European and American welfare states have in common and where they differ: facts and fiction in comparisons of the European Social Model and the United States', *Journal of European Social Policy*, 20(2): 102–25.

Alcock, P. and May, M. (2014) *Social Policy in Britain* (4th edn), Basingstoke: Palgrave Macmillan.

Alexander, A. (2009) *Britain's New Towns: Garden Cities to Sustainable Communities*, London: Routledge.

Amin, A. (2002) 'Ethnicity and the multicultural city: living with diversity', report for the Department of Transport, Local Government and the Regions and the ESRC Cities Initiative. Available at: http://citeseerx.ist.psu.edu/viewdoc/download?doi=10.1.1.378.3101&rep=rep1&type=pdf. Last accessed: 5 March 2016.

Barke, M. and Turnbull, G. (1992) *Meadowell: The Biography of an Estate with Problems*, Aldershot: Avebury.

Barker, N. (2017) 'Revealed: the scale of ex-RTB home conversions to private rent', *Inside Housing*. Available at: https://www.insidehousing.co.uk/insight/insight/revealed-the-scale-of-ex-rtb-home-conversions-to-private-rent-53525. Last accessed: 2 August 2018.

Barnes, S. (2017) 'Landlords tighten up affordability criteria under lower benefit cap', *Inside Housing*. Available at: https://www.insidehousing.co.uk/news/rising-stars-2017-entries-now-open-49748. Last accessed: 4 August 2018.

Battiston, D., Dickens, R., Manning, A. and Wadsworth, A. (2014) 'Immigration and the access to social housing in the UK', CEP Discussion Paper No 1264, London School of Economics. Available at: http://cep.lse.ac.uk/pubs/download/dp1264.pdf. Last accessed: 5 July 2016.

Becker, H. (1970) *Sociological Work: Method and Substance*, Chicago: Aldine Publishing Company.

Becker, S.O. and Fetzer, T. (2018) 'Has Eastern European migration impacted UK-born workers?', Warwick Economics Research Papers. Available at: https://warwick.ac.uk/fac/soc/economics/research/workingpapers/2018/twerp_1165_becker.pdf. Last accessed: 27 December 2018.

Beider, H. (2012) *Race, Housing and Community*, Chichester: Wiley-Blackwell.

Beider, H. (2014) 'Whiteness, class and grassroots perspectives on social change and difference', *The Political Quarterly*, 85(3): 333–9.

Beveridge, W.H.B. (1942) *Social Insurance and Allied Services. Report by Sir William Beveridge*, London: HMSO.

Birch, S., Gottfried, G. and Lodge, G. (2013) 'Divided democracy: political inequality in the UK and why it matters', Institute for Public Policy Research. Available at: www.ippr.org/files/images/media/files/publication/2013/11/divided-democracy_Nov2013_11420.pdf?noredirect=1. Last accessed: 18 August 2015.

Blair, T. (1997) cited in B. Lund (2017) *Understanding Housing Policy* (3rd edn), Bristol: Policy Press.

Blessing. A. (2016) Repackaging the poor? Conceptualising neoliberal reforms of social rental housing', *Housing Studies*, 31(2): 149–72.

Blyth, M. (2013) *Austerity: The History of a Dangerous Idea*, New York: Oxford University Press.

Bone, J. (2014) 'Neoliberal nomads: housing insecurity and the revival of private renting in the UK', *Sociological Research Online*, 19(4): 1.

Bottero, W. (2009) 'Class in the 21st Century', in K.P. Sveinsson (ed) *Who Cares about the White Working Class?* Runnymede Perspectives, pp 7–14. Available at: www.runnymedetrust.org/uploads/publications/pdfs/WhoCaresAboutTheWhiteWorkingClass-2009.pdf. Last accessed: August 2015.

Boughton, J. (2018a) 'Grenfell Tower and the long crisis of social housing', *Red Pepper*. Available at: https://www.redpepper.org.uk/grenfell-the-long-crisis-of-social-housing/. Last accessed: 4 August 2019.

Boughton, J. (2018b) *Municipal Dreams: The Rise and Fall of Council Housing*, London: Verso.

Bowie, D. (2017) *The Radical and Socialist Tradition in British Planning: From Puritan Colonies to Garden Cities*, London: Routledge.

Bradley, Q. (2014) *The Tenants' Movement: Resident Involvement, Community Action and the Contentious Politics of Housing*, New York: Routledge.

Bradshaw, J., Chzhen, Y. and Main, G. (2017) 'Impact of the recession on children in the United Kingdom', in B. Cantillon, Y. Chzhen, S. Handa and B. Nolan (eds) *Children of Austerity*, Oxford: United Nations Children's Fund and Oxford University Press, pp 275–96. Available at: https://www.unicef-irc.org/publications/pdf/Children_of_austerity.pdf. Last accessed: 10 January 2018.

Bragg, J., Burman, E., Greenstein, A., Hanley, T., Kalambouka, A., Lupton, R., McCoy, L., Spain, K. and Winter, L. (2015) 'The impact of the "Bedroom Tax" on children and their education: a study in the city of Manchester', University of Manchester. Available at: http://hummedia.manchester.ac.uk/schools/seed/education/research/projects/bedroom-tax/Bedroom-Tax-Final-Report.pdf. Last accessed: 10 January 2016.

Caraher, M. and Dowler. E. (2005) 'The great food divide'. Available at: http://news.bbc.co.uk/1/hi/business/4652801.stm. Last accessed: 18 January 2014.

Chance, W. (1917) *Industrial Unrest: The Reports of the Commissioners (July 1917) Collated and Epitomised*, London: P.S. King and Son, Ltd. Available at: https://ia902706.us.archive.org/19/items/industrialunres00unregoog/industrialunres00unregoog.pdf.

Cherrington, R. (2012) *Not Just Beer and Bingo! A Social History of Working Men's Clubs*, Bloomington: AuthorHouse.

Chossudovsky, M. and Marshall, A.G. (eds) (2010) *The Global Economic Crisis: The Great Depression of the XXI Century*, Montreal: Global Research.

CIH (Chartered Institute for Housing) (2018) 'Rethinking social housing: final report'. Available at: www.cih.org/resources/PDF/Policy%20free%20download%20pdfs/Final%20Rethinking%20social%20housing%20report.pdf. Last accessed: 4 January 2019.

Clarke, A., Hill, L., Marshall, B., Oxley, M., Pereira, I., Thomson, E. and Williams, P. (2015) 'Evaluation of the spare room subsidy: final report', Department for Work and Pensions Research Report No 913. Available at: https://www.gov.uk/government/uploads/system/uploads/attachment_data/file/506407/rsrs-evaluation.pdf. Last accessed: 10 December 2016.

Cole, I. (2007) 'What future for social housing in England?' *People, Place and Policy*, 1(1): 3–13.

Cole, I. and Furbey, R. (1994) *The Eclipse of Council Housing*, London: Routledge.

Cooper, N., Purcell, S. and Jackson, R. (2014) 'Below the breadline, the relentless rise of food poverty in Britain', Church Action on Poverty, Oxfam, the Trussell Trust. Available at: https://www.trusselltrust.org/wp-content/uploads/sites/2/2016/01/Below-the-Breadline-The-Trussell-Trust.pdf. Last accessed: 15 January 2015.

Cowen, D. and Marsh, A. (2001) 'New Labour, same old Tory housing policy?' *The Modern Law Review*, 64(2): 260–79.

Cowen, D. and Marsh, A. (forthcoming) *The Battle of the Bedroom Tax, A Study of Fairness and the Policy Process*, Bristol: Policy Press. Synopsis available at: https://www.bookdepository.com/Battle-Bedroom-Tax-Dave-Cowan/9781447327486. Last accessed: 3 January 2017.

Curtis, P. (2012) 'Will the housing benefit cap cause the "social cleansing" of London?', *The Guardian* [online]. Available at: https://www.theguardian.com/politics/reality-check-with-polly-curtis/2012/apr/24/housing-housing-benefit. Last accessed: 1 March 2013.

Davies, M. (nd) 'The pathologies of precarity', Newcastle University, EISA. Available at: www.eisa-net.org/be-bruga/eisa/files/events/warsaw2013/Davies_pathologies-of-precarity.pdf. Last accessed: 30 February 2016.

Delanty, G. (2010) *Community*, London and New York: Routledge.

Dench, G., Gavron, K. and Young, M. (2006) *The New East End: Kinship, Race and Conflict*, London: Profile Books.

Derbyshire, J. (2010) 'Poor relations', *New Statesman* [online]. Available at: https://www.newstatesman.com/uk-politics/2010/03/duncan-smith-social-interview. Last accessed: 21 August 2017.

Dorling, D. (2014) *All That Is Solid*, London: Penguin Books.

Dowler, E. (2014) 'Food banks and food justice in "austerity Britain"', in G. Riches and T. Silvasti (eds) *First World Hunger Revisited: Food Charity or the Right to Food?* Basingstoke: Palgrave Macmillan, 160–75.

Dowler, E., Turner, S. and Dobson, B. (2001) *Poverty Bites: Food, Health and Poor Families*, London: Child Poverty Action Group.

Duncan Smith, I. (2009) cited in T. Slater (2014) 'The myth of "Broken Britain": welfare reform and the production of ignorance', *Antipode*, 46: 948–69.

Duncan Smith, I. (2015) cited in 'Housing benefit bill rose by £2.4 billion under coalition as Labour claim new homes needed', *The Independent* [online]. Available at: https://www.independent.co.uk/news/uk/politics/generalelection/housing-benefit-bill-rose-by-24-billion-under-coalition-as-labour-claim-new-homes-needed-10108977.html. Last accessed: 1 August 2016.

Duncan Smith, I. (no date) 'The Centre for Social Justice (CSJ) Story'. Available at: https://www.centreforsocialjustice.org.uk/about/story. Last accessed: 20 August 2017.

Dwelly, T. and Cowans, J. (2006) (eds) 'Rethinking social housing', the Smith Institute. Available at www.smith-institute.org.uk/wp content/uploads/2015/11/RethinkingSocialHousing.pdf. Last accessed: 20 June 2016.

DWP (Department for Work and Pensions) (2010a) '21st century welfare', London: DWP. Available at www.dwp.gov.uk/docs/21st-century-welfare.pdf. Last accessed: 24 August 2014.

DWP (2010b) 'Universal Credit: welfare that works', London: DWP Available at: www.dwp.gov.uk/docs/universal-credit-full-document.pdf. Last accessed: 25 August 2014.

DWP (2012) 'Housing Benefit: under occupation of social housing Impact Assessment' (1A). Available at: https://www.gov.uk/government/uploads/system/uploads/attachment_data/file/229366/social-sector-housing-under-occupation-wr2011-ia.pdf. Last accessed: 24 August 2014.

ECSR (European Committee of Social Rights) (2014) European Social Charter, Conclusions XX-2 (2013) (Great Britain) Articles 3, 11, 12, 13 and 14 of the 1961 Charter.

EHRC (Equality and Human Rights Commission) (2018) 'The cumulative impact of tax and welfare reforms', *Equality and Human Rights Commission*. Available at: https://www.equalityhumanrights.com/sites/default/files/cumulative-impact-assessment-report-executive-summary.pdf. Last accessed: 4 February 2018.

Engels, F. (1845) 'Working class Manchester' (from *The Conditions of the Working Class in England in 1844*), in R. Tucker (1972/1978) *The Marx–Engels Reader* (2nd edn), London and New York: W.W. Norton & Company, pp 579–85.

Englander, D. (1979) 'Landlord and tenant in urban Britain: the politics of housing reform, 1838–1924', PhD thesis, University of Warwick. Available at: http://wrap.warwick.ac.uk/2821/1/WRAP_THESIS_Englander_1979.pdf. Last accessed: 20 August 2018.

Fetzer, T. (2018) 'Did austerity cause Brexit?', Working Paper Series No 381, Centre for Competitive Advantage in the Global Economy, Department of Economics. Available at: http://ukandeu.ac.uk/wp-content/uploads/2018/08/Did-Austerity-Cause-Brexit.pdf. Last accessed: 20 March 2019.

Fitzpatrick, S. and Pawson, H. (2014) 'Ending security of tenure for social renters: transitioning to "ambulance service" social housing?' *Housing Studies*, 29(5): 597–615.

Fitzpatrick, S., Pawson, H., Bramley, G., Wilcox, S. and Watts, B. (2015) 'The homelessness monitor: England 2015', London: Crisis. Available at: www.crisis.org.uk/data/files/publications/Homelessness_Monitor_England_2015_final_web.pdf. Last accessed: 16 March 2015.

Fitzpatrick, S., Pawson, H., Bramley, G., Wilcox, S. and Watts, B. (2017) 'The homeless monitor: England 2017', London: Crisis. Available at: https://crisis.org.uk/media/236823/homelessness_monitor_england_2017.pdf. Last accessed: 28 February 2018.

Forrest, A. and Murie, A. (1988) *Selling the Welfare State: The Privatisation of Public Housing*, London and New York: Routledge.

Fraser, D. (1973/1984) *The Evolution of the British Welfare State* (2nd edn), Basingstoke: Palgrave Macmillan.

Fraser, N, and Gordon, L. (1994) 'A Genealogy of Dependency: Tracing a Keyword of the U.S. Welfare State', *Signs*, 19(2): 309–36.

Fried, M. (1966) 'Grieving for a lost home: psychological costs of relocation', in Q.J. Wilson (ed) *Urban Renewal: The Record and the Controversy*, Cambridge, MA: M.I.T. Press, pp 359–79.

Fried, M. (2000) 'Continuities and discontinuities of place', *Journal of Environmental Psychology*, 20(3): 193–205.

Friedman, M. (1962/2002) *Capitalism and Freedom: Fortieth Anniversary Edition*, Chicago and London: University of Chicago Press.

Gamble, A. (1994) *The Free Economy and the Strong State: The Politics of Thatcherism* (2nd edn), Basingstoke: Palgrave Macmillan.

Garner, S. (2009) 'Home truths: the white working class and the racialization of social housing', in K.P. Sveinsson (ed) *Who Cares about the White Working Class?* Runnymede, pp 45–50. Available at: www.runnymedetrust.org/uploads/publications/pdfs/WhoCaresAboutTheWhiteWorkingClass-2009.pdf. Last accessed: 5 March 2015.

Garner, S. (2010) 'The entitled nation: how people make themselves white in contemporary Britain', *Sens Public*. Available at: www.sens-public.org/IMG/pdf/SensPublic_SGarner_entitled_nation.pdf. Last accessed: 7 March 2015.

Garner, S. (2011) 'White working-class neighbourhoods: common themes and policy suggestions', Joseph Rowntree Foundation. Available at: https://www.jrf.org.uk/report/white-working-class-neighbourhoods-common-themes-and-policy-suggestions. Last accessed: 5 March 2015.

Garner, S., Cowles, J., Lung, B. and Stott, M. (2009) 'Sources of resentment, and perceptions of ethnic minorities among poor white people in England', National Community Forum. Available at: http://resources.cohesioninstitute.org.uk/Publications/Documents/Document/DownloadDocumentsFile.aspx?recordId=9&file=PDFversion. Last accessed: 7 March 2015.

Garrett, P. (2015) 'Words Matter: Deconstructing "Welfare Dependency" in the UK', *Critical and Radical Social Work*, 3(3): 389–406.

Garthwaite, K. (2016) *Hunger Pains: Life inside Foodbank Britain*, Bristol: Policy Press.

Gibb, K. (2015) 'The multiple policy failings of the Bedroom Tax', *International Journal of Housing Policy*, 15(2): 148–66.

Greenhalgh, S. and Moss, J. (2009) 'Principles for social housing reform', Localis. Available at: www.localis.org.uk/wp-content/uploads/2009/04/localis-principles-for-social-housing-reform-web.pdf. Last accessed: 7 July 2014.

Grindrod, J. (2013) *Concretopia: A Journey around the Rebuilding of Postwar Britain*, Brecon: Old Street Publishing.

Gubrium, E., Pellissery, S. and Lodemel, I. (2014) (eds) *The Shame of It: Global Perspectives on Anti-Poverty Policies*, Bristol: Policy Press.

Hage, G. (2004) 'Migration, hope and the making of subjectivity in transnational capitalism', Ghassan Hage in conversation with Dimitris Papadopoulos, *Critical Psychology*, 12: 107–21. Available at: https://www2.le.ac.uk/departments/management/research/units/cppe/archiveactivities/texts/2004-Hage-Papadopoulos-IJCP.pdf. Last accessed: 20 September 2015.

Halewood, J. (2014) 'Official – DWP announce pre-1996 decision is true and thousands have had bedroom tax imposed in error!' *SPeye Joe (Welfarewrites)*. Available at: https://speye.wordpress.com/2014/01/08/official-dwp-announce-pre-1996-position-is-true-and-thousands-have-had-bedroom-tax-imposed-in-error/. Last accessed: 15 January 2014.

Hammersly, M. and Atkinson, P. (2007) *Ethnography: Principles in Practice* (3rd edn), London and New York: Routledge.

Hamnett, C. (2011) 'The reshaping of the British welfare system and its implications for geography and geographers', *Progress in Human Geography*, 35(2): 147–52.

Hancock, L. and Mooney, G. (2012) '"Welfare ghettos" and the "broken society": territorial stigmatization in the contemporary UK', *Housing, Theory and Society*, 30(1): 46–64.

Hancock, L., Mooney, G. and Neal, S. (2012) 'Crisis social policy and the resilience of the concept of community', *Critical Social Policy*, 32(3): 343–64.

Hanley, L. (2012) *Estates: An Intimate History*, London: Granta.

Harloe, M. (1995) *The People's Home? Social Rented Housing in Europe and America*, Oxford: Blackwell.

Harvey, D. (2005) *A Brief History of Neoliberalism*, Oxford: Oxford University Press.

Haylett, C. (2001) 'Illegitimate subjects? Abject whites, neoliberal modernisation, and middle-class multiculturalism', *Environment and Planning D: Society and Space*, 19(3): 351–70.

Henderson, J. and Karn, V. (1987) *Race, Class and State Housing: Inequality and the Allocation of Public Housing in Britain*, Aldershot: Gower.

Hewitt, R. (2005) *White Backlash and the Politics of Multiculturalism*, Cambridge: Cambridge University Press.

Hodkinson, S. and Robbins, G. (2013) 'The return of class war conservatism? Housing under the UK Coalition government', *Critical Social Policy*, 33(1): 57–77.

Hodkinson, S., Watt, P. and Mooney, G. (2013) 'Introduction: neoliberal housing policy – time for a critical re-appraisal', *Critical Social Policy*, 33(1), 3–16.

Hoggart, R. (1957/1992) *The Uses of Literacy*, London: Penguin Books.

Hollander, G. and Bury, R. (2012) 'Landlords braced for impact of benefit reform', *Inside Housing*. Available at: www.insidehousing.co.uk/ tenancies/landlords-braced-for-impact-of-benefit-reform/6520826. article. Last accessed: 13 December 2012.

Holmes, M. and Manning, N. (2013) '"Them that runs the country don't know what they're doing": political dissatisfaction amongst members of the white working class', *The Sociological Review*, 61(3): 479–98.

Iacobucci, G. (2014) 'GPs' workload climbs as government austerity agenda bites', *British Medical Journal*, 349: g4300.

Isaac, D. (2018) Quoted in Equality and Human Rights Commission (2018) 'One and a half million more children in poverty by 2022', *Equalityhumanrights.com*. Available at: https://www. equalityhumanrights.com/en/our-work/news/one-and-half-million-more-children-poverty-2022. Last accessed: 20 August 2019.

Jacobs, K., Kemeny, J. and Manzi, T. (2003) 'Power, discursive space and institutional practices in the construction of housing problems', *Housing Studies*, 1(4): 429–46.

Jessop, B. (2007) 'New Labour or the normalization of neo-liberalism?' *British Politics*, 2(2): 282–8.

Joyce, R. (2015) 'Benefit cuts: where might they come from?', Institute for Fiscal Studies. Available at: https://www.ifs.org.uk/ publications/7762. Last accessed: 2 June 2015.

Kemp, P.A. (2007) 'Housing allowances in Britain: a troubled history and uncertain future', in P.A. Kemp (ed) *Housing Allowances in Comparative Perspective*, Bristol: Policy Press, pp 105–34.

Kinnvall, C. (2004) 'Globalisation and religious nationalism: self, identity, and the search for ontological security', *Political Psychology*, 25(5): 741–67.

Lazarus, R.S. (1991) *Emotion and Adaptation*, New York: Oxford University Press.

Lee, H. (1974) *To Kill a Mockingbird*, London: Pan Books.

Lemke, T. (2001) 'The birth of bio-politics: Michel Foucault's lecture at the College de France on neo-liberal governmentality', *Economy and Society*, 30(2): 164–81.

Levitas, R. (2005) *The Inclusive Society? Social Exclusion and New Labour*, Basingstoke: Palgrave Macmillan.

Livingston, M., Bailey, N. and Kearns, A. (2008) 'People's attachment to place – the influence of neighbourhood deprivation', Joseph Rowntree Foundation. Available at: www.jrf.org.uk/sites/default/files/jrf/migrated/files/2200-neighbourhoods-attachment-deprivation.pdf. Last accessed:10 July 2015.

Loach, K. (2016) Cannes 2016: 'There's a conscious cruelty at the heart of Europe's welfare system'. Available at: https://www.youtube.com/watch?v=nitxAwd0Lp4. Last accessed: 25 May 2016.

Lorey, I. (2010) 'Becoming common: precarization as political constituting', *e-flux*. Available at: www.e-flux.com/journal/becoming-common-precarization-as-political-constituting/. Last accessed: 6 March 2015.

Lorey, I. (2015) *State of Insecurity: Government of the Precarious*, London and New York: Verso.

Lund, B. (2016) *Housing Politics in the United Kingdom: Power, Planning and Protest*, Bristol: Policy Press.

Malpass, P. and Murie, A. (1999) *Housing Policy and Practice* (5th edn), London: Macmillan.

Marris, P. (1974) *Loss and Change*, London: Routledge and Kegan Paul.

Marsh, A. (2014) 'The battle over the "Bedroom Tax": politics, rationality and discourse', paper presented at the European Network for Housing Research Conference *Beyond Globalisation: Remaking Housing Policy in a Complex World*, Edinburgh, July 2014.

Mayer, M. (2010) 'Punishing the poor – a debate: some questions on Wacquant's theorizing the neoliberal state', *Theoretical Criminology*, 14(1): 93–103.

McCafferty, S. (2012) 'Closing the door on the law: the implications for chronically sick and disabled tenants of the Housing Benefit (Amendment) regulations 2012', *We Are Spartacus*. Available at: http://wearespartacus.org.uk/wp-content/uploads/2012/07/Briefing-on-draft-Housing-Benefit-Amendment-Regulations-2012. pdf. Last accessed: 20 February 2013.

McKee, K., Muir, J. and Moore, T. (2017) 'Housing policy in the UK: the importance of spatial nuance', *Housing Studies*, 32(1): 60–72.

Mckenzie, L. (2015) *Getting By: Estates, Class and Culture in Austerity Britain*, Bristol: Policy Press.

Mckenzie, L. (2017) 'The Class System Is Static'. Available at: https://www.youtube.com/watch?v=oyL1tu0IiOM. Last accessed: 2 February 2018.

Mearns, A. (1883) *The Bitter Cry of Outcast London: An Inquiry into the Condition of the Abject Poor*, London: James Clarke and Co. Available at: https://archive.org/details/bittercryofoutca00pres. Last accessed: 12 March 2018.

Ministry of Housing Communities and Local Government 'English Housing Survey, Social Rented Sector 2016–17'. Available at: https://assets.publishing.service.gov.uk/government/uploads/system/uploads/attachment_data/file/724322/Social_rented_sector_report. pdf. Last accessed: 1 August 2018.

Moffatt, S., Lawson, S., Patterson, R., Holding, E., Dennison, A., Sowden, S. and Brown, J. (2015) 'A qualitative study of the impact of the UK "bedroom tax"', *Journal of Public Health*, 37(2): 1–9.

Mooney, G. (2008) 'Urban nightmares and dystopias, or places of hope?' *Variant*, 33: 14–6. Available at: http://oro.open.ac.uk/17750/1/Urban_Nightmares.pdf. Last accessed: 1 July 2016.

Mooney, G. and Neal, S. (2009) (eds) *Community: Welfare, Crime and Society*, Maidenhead: Open University Press.

Morrison, A. (1896) *A Child of the Jago* (3rd edn), London: Methuen & Co. Available at: www.gutenberg.org/files/36958/36958-h/36958-h. htm. Last accessed: 22 August 2018.

Mulligan, M. (2015) 'On ambivalence and hope in the restless search for community: how to work with the idea of community in the global age', *Sociology*, 49(2): 340–55.

Murie, A. (1997) 'The social rented sector, housing and the welfare state in the UK', *Housing Studies*, 12(4): 437–61.

Murray, C. (1990) *The Emerging British Underclass*, London: IEA Health and Welfare Unit.

Murray, C. (2009) 'Stigma makes generosity feasible', American Enterprise Institute. Available at: https://www.aei.org/publication/stigma-makes-generosity-feasible/. Last accessed: 10 February 2016.

NAO (National Audit Office) (2017) 'Homelessness', Department for Communities and Local Government. Available at: https://www.nao.org.uk/wp-content/uploads/2017/09/Homelessness.pdf. Last accessed: 24 February 2018.

Nevitt, A.A. (1977) 'Housing in a Welfare State', *Urban Studies*, 14(1): 33–40.

NHF (National Housing Federation) (2016) 'Older people, disabled people and most vulnerable to lose £68 a week in housing benefit', NHF Press Releases, 26 January. Available at: www.housing.org.uk/press/press-releases/older-people-disabled-people-and-most-vulnerable-to-lose-68-a-week/. Last accessed: 1 February 2016.

Nowicki, M. (2014) 'Rethinking Domicide: Towards an expanded critical geography of home', *Geography Compass*, 8(11): 785–95.

O'Malley, P. (2010) 'Resilient subjects: uncertainty, warfare and liberalism', *Economy and Society*, 39(4): 488–509.

Paton, K. (2013) HSA Special Issue: 'Housing in "hard times": marginality, inequality and class', *Housing, Theory and Society*, 30(1): 84–100.

Paton, K. and Cooper, V. (2016) 'It's the state, stupid: 21st gentrification and state-led evictions', *Sociological Research Online*, 21(3): 1–7.

Peacock, M., Bissell, P. and Owen, J. (2013) 'Shaming encounters: reflections on contemporary understandings of social inequality and health', *Sociology*, 48(2): 387–402.

Peacock, M., Bissell, P. and Owen, J. (2014) 'Dependency denied: health inequalities in the neo-liberal era', *Social Science & Medicine*, 118: 173–80.

Pearce, J. and Vine, J. (2014) 'Quantifying residualisation: the changing nature of social housing in the UK', *Journal of Housing and the Built Environment*, 29(4): 657–75.

Peck, J. (2001) *Workfare States*, New York and London: Guildford Press.

Peck, J. (2013) 'Explaining (with) neoliberalism', *Territory, Politics, Governance*, 1(2): 132–57.

Peck, J. and Tickell, A. (2002) 'Neoliberalizing space', *Antipode*, 34(3): 380–404.

Phillips, D., Athwal, B., Harrison, M., Robinson, D., Bashir, N. and Atkinson, J. (2010) 'Neighbourhood, community and housing in Bradford: building understanding between new and settled groups', Joseph Rowntree Foundation. Available at: https://www.jrf.org. uk/sites/default/files/jrf/migrated/files/Bradford-communities-neighbourhoods-full.pdf. Last accessed: 24 July 2016.

Pierson, P. (2002) 'Coping with permanent austerity: welfare state restructuring in affluent democracies', *R. Franc. Social*, 43(2): 369–406.

Pilkington, H., (2014) '"Loud and proud": youth activism in the English Defence League', WP7: Interpreting Activism (Ethnographies). Deliverable 7.1: Ethnographic Case Studies of Youth Activism, *MYPLACE Deliverable Report*. Available at: http://www.fp7-myplace. eu/deliverables.php. Last accessed: 19 December 2015.

Pilkington, H. (2016) *Loud and Proud: Passion and Politics in the English Defence League*, Manchester: Manchester University Press.

Porteous, J.D. and Smith, S.E. (2001) *Domicide: The Global Destruction of Home*, Montreal and Kingston: McGill-Queen's University Press.

Power, A. (1997) *Estates on the Edge: The Social Consequences of Mass Housing in Northern Europe*, Basingstoke: Macmillan.

Procter, I. (June 1990) 'The privatisation of working-class life: a dissenting view', *The British Journal of Sociology*, 41(2): 157–80.

Ravetz, A. (2001) *Council Housing and Culture: The History of a Social Experiment*, New York: Routledge.

Rex, J. and Moore, R. (1967) *Race, Community, and Conflict: A Study of Sparkbrook*, New York: Oxford University Press.

Rhodes, J. (2011) '"It's not just them, it's whites as well": whiteness, class and BNP support', *Sociology*, 45(1): 102–17.

Riches, G. (1997) *First World Hunger, Food Security and Welfare Politics*, Basingstoke: Macmillan.

Riches, G. and Silvasti, T. (2014) (eds) *First World Hunger Revisited: Food Charity or the Right to Food?* (2nd edn), Basingstoke: Palgrave Macmillan.

Ridge, T. (2011) 'The everyday costs of poverty in childhood: a review of qualitative research exploring the lives and experiences of low-income children in the UK', *Children and Society*, 25(1): 73–84.

Robinson, D. (2008) 'New immigrants and migrants in social housing in England', Centre for Regional Economic and Social Research, Sheffield Hallam University. Available at: www.local.gov. uk/c/document_library/get_file?uuid=6a03ed1e-6fbd-4bfc-91cc-031018966cca&groupId=10180. Last accessed: 10 March 2016.

Robinson, D. and Reeve, K. (2006) 'Neighbourhood experiences of new immigration: reflections on the evidence base', Joseph Rowntree Foundation. Available at: https://www.jrf.org.uk/report/experiences-new-immigration-neighbourhood-level. Last accessed: 23 July 2016.

Rolnik, R. (2013) 'Report of the Special Rapporteur on adequate housing as a component of the right to an adequate standard of living, and on the right to non-discrimination in this context', United Nations General Assembly, Human Rights Council Twenty-Fifth Session, Agenda Item 3.

Ruskin, M. (2010) 'From the beginning to the end of neo-liberalism in Britain', *OpenDemocracy UK*. Available at: https://www.opendemocracy.net/ourkingdom/mike-rustin/after-neo-liberalism-in-britain. Last accessed: 5 January 2019.

Rutter, J. and Latorre, M. (2009) 'Social housing allocation and immigrant communities', Research Report 4 Migration, Equalities and Citizenship Team, Institute for Public Policy Research, Equality and Human Rights Commission. Available at https://www.equalityhumanrights.com/sites/default/files/research_report_4_social_housing_allocation_and_immigrant_communities.pdf. Last accessed: 14 June 2016.

Sayer, A. (2005) 'Class, moral worth and recognition', *Sociology*, 39(5): 947–63.

Sennett, R. and Cobb, J. (1973) *The Hidden Injuries of Class*, New York: Vintage Books.

Sheff, T.J. (2000) 'Shame and the social bond: a sociological theory', *Sociological Theory*, 18(1): 84–99.

Shelter (2017) 'Shut out: The barriers low-income households face in private renting' *Shelter.org.uk*. Available at: https://england.shelter.org.uk/__data/assets/pdf_file/0004/1391701/2017_06_-_Shut_out_the_barriers_low_income_households_face_in_pivate_renting.pdf. Last accessed: 20 April 2018.

Shildrick, T. and MacDonald, R. (2013) 'Poverty talk: how people experiencing poverty deny their poverty and why they blame "the poor"', *The Sociological Review*, 61(2): 285–303.

Shildrick, T., MacDonald, R., Webster, C. and Garthwaite, K. (2012) *Poverty and Insecurity: Life in Low-Pay, No-Pay Britain*, Bristol: Policy Press.

Skeggs, B. (2004) *Class, Self, Culture*, London and New York: Routledge.

Skeggs, B. (2009) 'Haunted by the spectre of judgement: respectability, value and affect in class relations', in K.P. Sveinsson (ed) *Who Cares about the White Working Class?* Runnymede, pp 36–44. Available at: www.runnymedetrust.org/uploads/publications/pdfs/WhoCaresAboutTheWhiteWorkingClass-2009.pdf. Last accessed: 29 February 2013.

Skey, M. (2012) 'Interview with Dr Michael Skey', *Studies in Ethnicity and Nationalism*. Available at: http://senjournal.co.uk/2012/04/23/interview-with-dr-michael-skey/. Last accessed: 14 January 2016.

Skey, M. (2014) '"How do you think I feel? It's my country": belonging, entitlement and the politics of immigration', *The Political Quarterly*, 85(3): 326–32.

Slater, T. (2013) 'Grieving for a lost home revisited: the 'Bedroom Tax' and displacement', *The University of Edinburgh, School of Geosciences*. Available at: http://www.geos.ed.ac.uk/homes/tslater/bedroomtax.html. Last accessed: 20 January 2015.

Sprigings, N. and Smith, D.H. (2012) 'Unintended consequences: local housing allowance meets the right to buy', *People, Place and Policy*, 6(2): 58–75.

State of the Nation (2014) 'Social mobility and child poverty in Great Britain', Social Mobility and Child Poverty Commission. Available at: https://assets.publishing.service.gov.uk/government/uploads/system/uploads/attachment_data/file/365765/State_of_Nation_2014_Main_Report.pdf. Last accessed: 12 August 2016.

Stephens, M. (2005) 'An assessment of the British Housing Benefit system', *European Journal of Housing Policy*, 5(2): 111–29.

Tate, A. (2012) 'Briefing, Welfare Reform Act 2012: size criteria', National Housing Federation. Available at: www.housing.org.uk/publications/find_a_publication/legislation/welfare_reform_act_2012.aspx. Last accessed: 12 September 2012.

Taylor-Gooby, P. (2004) 'New Risks and Social Change' in P. Taylor-Gooby (ed) *New Risks, New Welfare: The Transformation of the European Welfare State*, New York: Oxford University Press, 1–28.

Taylor-Gooby, P. (2016) 'The divisive welfare state', *Social Policy & Administration*, 50(6): 712–33.

Taylor-Gooby, P. and Stoker, G. (2011) 'The Coalition Programme: A New Vision for Britain or Politics as Usual?' *The Political Quarterly*, 82(1): 4–14.

Titmuss, R.M. (1950) *Problems of Social Policy*, London: HMSO.

Torgersen, U. (1987) 'Housing: the wobbly pillar under the welfare state', *Scandinavian Journal of Housing and Planning Research Supplement*, 4(1): 116–27.

Trentelman, C.K. (2009) 'Place attachment and community attachment: a primer grounded in the lived experience of a community sociologist', *Society & Natural Resources*, 22(3): 191–210.

Tyler, I. (2008) '"Chav mum, chav scum": class disgust in contemporary Britain', *Feminist Media Studies*, 8(1):17–34.

Tyler, I. (2015) *Revolting Subjects: Social Abjection and Resistance in Neoliberal Britain*, London and New York: Zed Books.

UNICEF (2014) 'Children of the recession, the impact of the economic crisis on child well-being in rich countries', Innocenti Report Card 12. Available at: https://www.unicef-irc.org/publications/pdf/rc12-eng-web.pdf. Last accessed: 20 January 2015.

Venkatesh, S. (2008) *Gang Leader for a Day*, London: Penguin Books.

Wacquant, L. (1996) 'The rise of advanced marginality: notes on its nature and implications', *Acta Sociologica*, 39(2): 121–39.

Wacquant, L. (1999) 'Urban marginality in the coming millennium', *Urban Studies*, 36(10): 1639–47.

Wacquant, L. (2007) 'Territorial stigmatization in the age of advanced marginality', *Thesis Eleven*, 91(1): 66–77.

Wacquant, L. (2008) *Urban Outcasts: A Comparative Sociology of Advanced Marginality*, Cambridge: Polity Press.

Wacquant, L. (2009) *Punishing the Poor*, Durham, NC and London: Duke University Press.

Wacquant, L. (2012) 'Three steps to a historical anthropology of actually existing neoliberalism', *Social Anthropology*, 20(1): 66–77.

Wacquant, L. (2013) 'Constructing neoliberalism: opening salvo', *Nexus*. Available at: http://loicwacquant.net/assets/Papers/openingsalvoonneoliberalism.NexusPub.pdf. Last accessed: 13 January 2015.

Walker, R. (2014) *The Shame of Poverty*, Oxford: Oxford University Press.

Walker, R. and Chase, E. (2014) 'Separating the sheep from the goats: tackling poverty in Britain for over four centuries', in E. Gubrium, S. Pellissery and I. Lodomel (eds) *The Shame of It: Global Perspectives on Anti-Poverty Policies*, Bristol: Policy Press, pp 133–56.

Ward, K. (2008) 'Local experiences of migration: consulting Coventry', Information Centre for Asylum and Refugees (ICAR). Available at: http://icar.livingrefugeearchive.org/Cov1.pdf. Last accessed: 12 January 2016.

Wasoff, F. (1998) 'Women and Housing', in I. Shaw, S. Lambert and D. Clapham (eds) *Research Highlights in Social Work 32, Social Care and Housing*, London and Philadelphia: Jessica Kingsley Publishers, pp 127–44.

We Are Spartacus (2012) 'The hardest hit: the people's review of the work capability assessment'. Available at: http://wearespartacus.org.uk/wp-content/uploads/2012/11/The-Peoples-Review-of-the-Work-Capability-Assessment.pdf. Last accessed: 12 February 2013.

Webb, K. (2012) 'Bricks or benefits? Rebalancing housing investment', executive summary, Shelter. Available at: https://england.shelter.org.uk/__data/assets/pdf_file/0010/436276/Bricksorbenefitsexecsummary.pdf. Last accessed: 12 April 2015.

Webster, C. (2008) 'Marginalized white ethnicity, race and crime', *Theoretical Criminology*, 12(93): 293–312.

Wiggan, J. (2012) 'Telling stories of 21st century welfare: the UK Coalition government and the neo-liberal discourse of worklessness and dependency', *Critical Social Policy*, 32(3): 383–405.

Wilcox, S., Perry, J. and Williams, P. (2015) 'UK Housing Review', 2015 Briefing Paper, Chartered Institute of Housing. Available at: www.cih.org/resources/PDF/Policy%20free%20download%20pdfs/UKHR%20Briefing%202015.pdf. Last accessed: 3 January 2017.

Wilding, P. (1972) 'Towards Exchequer Subsidies for Housing 1906–1914', *Social Policy & Administration*, 6(1): 3–18.

Wilkinson, R.G. (1996) *Unhealthy Societies: The Afflictions of Inequality*, London and New York: Routledge.

Wilkinson, R.G. and Pickett, K. (2009) *The Spirit Level: Why Equality Is Better for Everyone*, London: Penguin Books.

Winlow, S., Hall, S. and Treadwell, J. (2017) *The Rise of the Right. English Nationalism and the Transformation of Working-Class Politics*, Bristol: Policy Press.

Wood, C. and Grant, E. (2010) 'Destination unknown', Demos. Available at: www.demos.co.uk/files/Destination_unknown_-_web.pdf?1286894260. Last accessed: 27 March 2013.

Wrenn, M.V. (18 June 2014) 'The social ontology of fear and neoliberalism', *Review of Social Economy*, 72(3): 337–53.

Yuval-Davis, N., Anthias, F. and Kofman, E. (2005) 'Secure borders and safe haven and the gendered politics of belonging: beyond social cohesion', *Ethnic and Racial Studies*, 28(3): 513–35.

Index

Benefit Street (TV show) 98, 99
benefit scroungers 30
Beveridge, William 22, 23
Big Society 12, 139, 153
The Bitter Cry of Outcast London (Mearns)
  16
Blair, Tony 28–9, 30
Blessing, A. 36
Blyth, Mark 31–2, 33
BNP (British National Party) 117
Boundary Street estate 19
Britain
  Commonwealth citizens 25
  postwar reconstruction of 24
  underclass 29
Brown, Gordon 1
budget deficit 112–13
  see also austerity

C
Cameron, David 115, 116–17
Central Labour College Movement 21
Centre for Social Justice 29
Chartist Convention 17
Cherrington, Ruth 129–30
child poverty 63, 67
class 18
  positions 99
  see also working classes
Coalition government (2010–2015) 1,
  32–5
  austerity programme 145
  reducing the national debt 33
Committee on Social Rights report
  (2014) 45
community 125–43
  ambiguity of 139
  clinging on to 126–32
  crucial social bonds 153
  dark side of 140
  fear of being taken away 136
  fear of displacement 131–43
  funeral costs 129
  informal caring practices 127–8,
    135
  length of residence 127
  notions of 125
  ontological anchorage 135

place attachment 125, 127, 135–6,
  138–9, 154
proximity to family and friends 128
responsibility for fostering mutual
  responsibility and self-help 139
tangible benefits 129
women's mutual support networks
  135
see also belonging; displacement
community integration 118–22
computer literacy 78
condition tests 80–2, 149
The Conditions of the Working Class in
  England in 1844 (Engels) 16
Conservative Party 2, 3
  election victory (2015) 35
  Housing Benefit changes 155
  rhetoric of Big Society 139
Construction Skills Certification Scheme
  (CSCS) 115
council estates 24
  Easterhouse 29
  perceived as problem places 29
  Radburn layout 24, 39
  stereotyping of 30–1
  stigmatisation of 146
  Tarley estate see Tarley estate
council housing 145
  benefits for working classes 10–11
  Black and Ethnic Minority sector 25
  building programmes 21–2
  depleted stock of 26
  discrimination 25
  discriminatory allocation 22–3
  growth 9
  intra-class struggles over 23
  and New Labour 28–32
  privatisation of 26
  and RSLs 26
  sales of houses 26, 27, 30
  security of tenure 27
  stereotyping of 30–1
  stock transfers to housing associations
    30
  successes 31
  tainted image of 29
  see also RTB (Right to Buy); social
    housing